BURREN ARCHAEOLOGY

HUGH CARTHY developed an interest in everything
to do with the Burren after moving to County Clare in 1992.
He had studied archaeology for two years at NUI Galway
during his degree programme in 1976–79.
In 2008 he obtained an Hons. Diploma in Archaeology
from NUIG, dealing specifically with the Burren
and the Aran Islands. He now provides guided tours
from his base in Ennis, County Clare

www.burrenarchaeology.ie

All houses wherein men have lived and died
Are haunted houses. Through the open doors
The harmless phantoms on their errands glide,
With feet that make no sound upon the floors.

'Haunted Houses,' Henry Wadsworth Longfellow

BURREN ARCHAEOLOGY
A TOUR GUIDE

HUGH CARTHY

The Collins Press

FIRST PUBLISHED IN 2011 BY
The Collins Press
West Link Park
Doughcloyne
Wilton
Cork

British Library Cataloguing in Publication Data
Carthy, Hugh.
Burren archaeology : a tour guide.
1. Burren (Ireland)—Antiquities. 2. Megalithic
monuments—Ireland—Burren. 3. Burren (Ireland)—
Guidebooks.
I. Title
936.1'93-dc22

ISBN-13: 9781848891050

Design and typesetting by Illuminate
Typeset in Adobe Garamond
Printed in Italy by Printer Trento

All photographs courtesy of the author except where credited differently.
Photograph on pp. ii–iii: Poulnabrone dolmen (courtesy Jean Von Trende).

Contents

Preface

The plan was to write a two-page introduction to the archaeology of the Burren for a tourism website. Reading the completed draft, I realised there were a few things I had omitted, and so two pages became three. Eighteen months and many hours of fascinated research later, this is the result!

I have thought about many things while writing this guidebook – the vastness of time, the resilience of people, the capacity of the human race for construction and destruction, the beauty of architecture and the almost incredible acceleration in our acquisition of knowledge. More than anything else, however, I have been struck by a sense of wonder when I've thought about the people who have been shaping our world for millennia. Real people lived here and hauled rocks across the landscape to build memorials for their dead and houses for their families. Real people carved and hammered intricate designs onto animal bones and sheets of gold. Real people spent months travelling all over Europe to trade, build, pray, marry, conspire and fight. Most had no concept of the twenty-first century, and yet their memory survives in our world. It is all around us, but it is easy to miss, ignore or to underestimate its significance. This is a shameful omission.

The fact that our ancestors were building small wedge tombs at precisely the same time that the Egyptians were creating enormous pyramids does not in any way diminish their achievements or dilute their contribution to what we have become today. They are in our genes – relevant in a way they could never have imagined and that we too often fail to appreciate.

The Burren is a fascinating place for all sorts of reasons. Geology and hydrology combine to produce a unique landscape that has inspired poets and painters. Biology and chemistry work unseen to produce a unique environment for the people who continue to work the land millennia after the first farmers arrived. History, politics and religion have superimposed a story that needs to be told. My aim in writing this guidebook has been to persuade the visitor to read the story. Archaeological monuments are not isolated features in the landscape – they are integral parts *of* a landscape that includes physical and cultural components that cannot and should not be separated. If it does nothing more than give the reader pause to wonder, this book will have served its purpose.

Monuments described in the book are grouped by location – north, east, west and central – with accompanying maps to assist the visitor in planning manageable itineraries. The sequence of monuments listed in the book follows the routes suggested on the maps. The area is too big, and there are too many monuments, to visit in one day. However, I recognise that some visitors will have only a short while to stay in the Burren and will need to be selective. The maps should help in such cases.

I am grateful for the assistance and encouragement of many people who helped produce this book. My wife, Agnes, has shown exemplary patience – no more need be said! My daughter, Nicola, waded through drafts of the text, helped to 'road-test' the monument descriptions and designed the access graphics. My son, Mark, got up before dawn one morning to take some great photographs at Corcomroe Abbey. Noel Dunne reviewed Part 1 and provided very useful comments and additional information. Christine Fazentieux translated research material from the original French. The Collins Press had the courage to take the project on and guide this neophyte through the publication process. Any faults, errors or omissions in the final draft are my responsibility alone.

No less than anybody else who researches the archaeology of the Burren today, I am hugely indebted to the surveyors, travel writers, antiquarians and archaeologists who have walked the roads, tracks and fields, and documented their findings since the middle of the nineteenth century. They have left an invaluable record. Professional archaeologists continue to make discoveries with each new excavation season. How they do not despair at the amount of work still to be done is beyond me. There is no substitute for eyeballing a monument when the sun is shining, but a special word of thanks is due to Clare County Council for the comprehensive online and library resources that they have gathered together on their website and at the Local Studies Centre in Ennis. These take care of the rainy days!

I am also grateful to the many landowners who gave me permission to visit monuments on their properties. Without their enthusiasm and goodwill many of the archaeological treasures of the Burren would be inaccessible, and an important part of our heritage would remain hidden away.

The book includes many references to research sources and published material. The casual reader can safely ignore these notes without fear of missing any additional explanatory information. For those readers who wish to delve further into the sources, a full bibliography is included at the end of the book.

All photographs are copyright of the author except where stated otherwise.

Access to Monuments

Whilst many of the monuments described in this guide are open to the public, others are located on private property. The Burren is home to a vibrant community that continues to work and manage the land millennia after the first farmers arrived. Their property rights must be respected by visitors. To help the visitor, each site description in this book includes a symbol indicating the site's access status:

 Public. The site is open to the public.

 Private, visible. The site is on private property but can be seen from a public space. To visit the site, the owner's permission should be sought.

 Private. The site is not visible from a public space and can only be seen by crossing private property. Very few of the monuments described are in this category but they are included here for their importance and cultural significance. Landowners' permission should be sought before visiting.

The fact that a monument is described or included on a map in this guidebook does not necessarily imply that there is a right of way to it. The Author and Publisher disclaim any responsibility for loss, damage, injury or inconvenience sustained by users of the guidebook.

Landowners in the Burren are proud of our common heritage. Many see themselves as custodians of the vast array of monuments that dot the landscape and are happy for visitors to view monuments on their properties, provided always that they have the courtesy to ask for permission and avoid damaging property, leaving gates open etc. There are legitimate reasons why permission may at times be refused, for example in the presence of livestock or while farm machinery is being operated, but in general these monuments are accessible through the continuing goodwill of landowners. Visitors should avoid doing anything that might erode that goodwill.

Brief mention needs to be made about terrain in the Burren. The area is characterised by weathered limestone pavement that can present difficulties for the visitor. Limestone slabs (known as clints) can be loose underfoot, and the cracks between clints (known as grykes) can be deep. Extreme care is needed when crossing open terrain, especially when it is overgrown, as deep grykes can be concealed.

Sunset in the Burren

Introduction

There is an abundance of archaeological remains to be seen throughout Ireland. In most parts of the country, however, you can travel for miles without noticing any, except perhaps for the occasional 'castle' or tower house. The Burren is different; you will not travel very far here without coming across something that catches your eye and prompts you to ask 'What's that?'

Part 1 of this guidebook provides a brief introduction to the archaeology of the Burren. Part 2 gives descriptions of some of the more interesting and accessible monuments that can be seen in the area. Many of these are National Monuments and are accessible year round to the public. Some, however, are on private property and are accessible only with the permission and continuing goodwill of the landowners who live and work here. The fact that a description appears in this book should not be taken as a guarantee that the monument is accessible to the public and you are advised to respect the wishes and directions of the landowners concerned. In general, any monument that is signposted may be visited by the public.

Throughout Ireland today, many place names derive from their original form in the Irish language. Indeed, a study of these place names is now an integral part of much archaeological research. As an aid to pronunciation for those visitors unfamiliar with the language, phonetic spellings will be included in square brackets in this guide where appropriate, e.g. *Cabhail Tighe Breac* [kowil chee brack]. In some cases, Irish and English versions will be used interchangeably.

The Burren is a 36,000 hectare (140 square miles) karst region in north County Clare. Karst is rough limestone terrain with underground drainage, and it is the interaction of water and limestone through the Ice Ages and since the end of the last Ice Age 12,000 years ago that gives the area its distinctive appearance and characteristics. The upland topography and abundance of surface rock have contributed in no small way to ensuring that the Burren has one of the densest concentrations of archaeology in the country – a treasure trove that traces the history of human habitation and activity since shortly after the first arrival of people to this country 9,500 years ago.

The name 'Burren' derives from the Irish word *boireann* [bwirenn], which means 'a rocky hill' or 'a stony place'.1 The term was used descriptively until the sixteenth century and referred to an area formerly controlled by the dominant tribal group known as the *Corcu Modruadh* [kurku mruah]. This area was divided under the English system of administration into two baronies – Corcomroe in the west and Burren in the east. Modern usage has more or less reverted to the original descriptive form and the term now refers broadly to the area north of the road from Corrofin through Kilfenora to Doolin. The eastern boundary is less well defined. The lowlands west of the town of Gort in County Galway are characteristically karstic, but for the purposes of this guide only those parts of the Burren in County Clare will be included.

PART 1

The Archaeological Ages

It is unfortunate that prehistoric and early historic times have been divided into convenient slices, as outlined in the table below. Such neat divisions are misleading because they give the impression of sudden transformations from one 'culture' to the next. The transformation from Mesolithic society (typically of the hunter-gatherer form) to Neolithic (the first farmers), though dated by convention in Ireland to 4000 BC, may have taken place over a period of many centuries. There is evidence of Mesolithic and Neolithic groupings living side by side over many generations in County Mayo, for example. The conventional divisions are well established, however, and will be used extensively in the following pages.

Archaeological Period	Date range
Palaeolithic	Before c. 7500 BC
Mesolithic	7500–4000 BC
Neolithic	4000–2400 BC
Bronze Age	2400–600 BC
Iron Age	600 BC – AD 400
Early Medieval/Early Christian	AD 400–1169
Medieval	AD 1169–c. 1530

Palaeolithic (before c. 7500 BC)

Strictly speaking, there does not appear to have been a Palaeolithic period in Ireland. The term derives from the very earliest forms of stone implements manufactured or modified for use by early humans. These were crudely made, probably for immediate use, and may have been discarded when the task for which they were made was completed. At present, there is no firm evidence for any human activity in Ireland until about 7500 BC. This seems strange, given that human activity has been recorded in Britain as early as 500,000 years ago. It may be that evidence for early activity, if it exists at all, has not yet been discovered in Ireland or has been erased from the landscape by glacial or geological activity. All we can say for certain is that, on present evidence, humans first began to leave their mark on the Irish landscape nearly 10,000 years ago.

Much was going on before the arrival of the first humans, however, that is relevant to the Burren as we see it today.

The last Ice Age ended 10,000 to 12,000 years ago. During one of the mini-thaws (known as interstadials) that occurred during this glacial period, animals that are now extinct, such as woolly mammoth and giant Irish deer, roamed the land. Brown bears were also present and they probably hibernated in the many caves of the Burren during the winter. These caves continued to be used by bears right up to the Early Christian period, and the remains of one can still be seen at Aillwee Cave, a few kilometres south of Ballyvaghan.

Temperatures rose rapidly following the retreat of the ice, and the whole of Western Europe warmed dramatically over a period of about nine years c. 8200 BC.[1] From c. 6000–4000 BC, the average temperature was about 1 to 2 degrees higher than today.This was the period during which Ireland was covered by vast forests, initially of pine and hazel and later of oak and elm. In the west of Ireland, from Mayo through Connemara to the Burren, pine forests persisted until about 2000 BC.

Mesolithic (7500–4000 BC)

This vast forest was the landscape that greeted the first people to arrive in Ireland, probably shortly before 7500 BC. Who they were and where they came from is unclear. It used to be thought that they arrived across a land bridge connecting Scotland with County Antrim in the northeast corner of Ireland, at a time when sea levels were lower due to the vast amounts of water locked in the polar ice caps. From there they expanded southwards, eventually reaching the southernmost parts of Ireland by about 5500 BC. There are particular reasons why this theory gained prominence; for example, much of the early research on the archaeology of Mesolithic settlements in Ireland was done in Ulster. Many of the earliest recognised Mesolithic artefacts were also discovered there. It is only more recently that southern sites have begun to be recognised and investigated. The northeastern land bridge theory may be accurate, but there are other possibilities for the arrival of the first people in Ireland.

One such possibility is that they arrived in the south of the country as a result of expanding maritime trading networks. We appear seriously to have underestimated the extent and importance of coastal trade routes throughout the prehistory of Western Europe, perhaps flippantly dismissing our ancestors as primitive hunter-gatherers. Sea levels at the beginning of the Mesolithic period were 10–16 m lower than today, making for shorter sea journeys between land masses. Fish was also very important in the diet of the earliest settlers. This is clear from the fact that 70–80 per cent of bones recovered during excavation of Mesolithic coastal sites typically consist of fish. Woven Mesolithic fish baskets/traps have also been found in excavations at Clowanstown, County Meath (one dating to 5210–4970 BC). Another basket, from Carrigdirty Rock, County Limerick in the Shannon Estuary, returned a date of 3875–3535 BC. Mesolithic people are also known to have used seagoing dugout canoes. Part of one such canoe, recovered on the Shannon Estuary at Carrigdirty, County Limerick, has been dated to c. 4600 BC.

It is clear that people were living throughout the island of Ireland by the Late Mesolithic period, and although no clearly identifiable Mesolithic objects or remains have been discovered in the Burren, it is inconceivable that the area would not have been visited by groups of nomadic hunter-gatherers foraging for food. Availability of water (both marine and freshwater) was important for Mesolithic people, but whether they established in the Burren any of the seasonal coastal settlements, or 'base camps', that were typical of the period remains to be seen. The absence of permanent lakes and streams in the Burren may have militated against the establishment of settled or semi-settled communities in the area, although drainage patterns may well have been different then.

There are hints of Mesolithic activity near the Burren. Lake Inchiquin, near Corrofin, is at the southern edge of the Burren, and a number of potentially Mesolitic objects such as stone axes and a perforated deer antler have been found there. A stone 'axe factory' at the mouth of the River Aille in Fisherstreet near Doolin produced similar stone tools. Interestingly, but not surprisingly, this area is also at the southern extremity of the Burren, where the limestone pavement slips under the shale layers – an obvious source for shale tools. The presence of a court tomb nearby indicates that the area was a focus for human activity at least as far back as the Early Neolithic, but confirmation of a Mesolithic presence must await further study.

Neolithic (4000–2400 BC)

The Neolithic period is when people began to leave their mark on the Burren, and today this area has one of the densest concentrations of Neolithic remains in the country. There is clear evidence of habitation sites and more extensive settlements where people lived and engaged in animal husbandry and cereal production. They also built ritual monuments – lots of them – using large slabs of stone (megaliths). Many of these megalithic monuments are well preserved and clearly visible. Indeed, the Neolithic portal tomb at Poulnabrone (dating to about 3200 BC) is one of the most photographed and easily recognisable images of the Burren.

The contrasts between the Mesolithic and the Neolithic are striking. As well as the physical differences in tools, habitation sites and use of resources, a sea change occurred at the conceptual level. Mesolithic people were hunter-gatherers who roamed the land, settling only temporarily at seasonal base camps and with an apparently limited concept of ritual. Territory and ritual were sufficiently important in the Neolithic for people to invest a lot of time and energy in enclosing land and constructing large monuments. Why should this have been so, and how did the old order come eventually to be obliterated by the new?

It seems unlikely that the transition occurred spontaneously among resident Mesolithic people. The Mesolithic lifestyle had survived for millennia. There were plenty of resources available to support the small Mesolithic population, and while life expectancy was much shorter than today (possibly as little as thirty years), we can confidently speculate that theirs would have been a reasonably happy existence, if similar societies living today are anything to go by. (We should not make the common mistake of judging contentment by modern standards!)

Farming was already established in Southeast Europe by the time the first Mesolithic people arrived in Ireland around 7500 BC, and the spread of this new way of life can be traced generally northwestwards, reaching Ireland by about 4000 BC. In some parts of Europe, Neolithic groups settled in places where there had been no previous Mesolithic presence; in others, Mesolithic and Neolithic groups co-existed.

The Neolithic 'culture' probably arrived in Ireland, therefore, in the same way that everything else arrived – flora, fauna and the earliest people. It came slowly from the south or southeast, introducing to resident populations a different view of the world. They had a different concept of time and were more aware of their ancestors. They were also better able to plan for the future, with permanent settlements becoming the norm and tools reused to a greater extent than before. New plants and animals were also introduced, with domesticated cattle and cereals the mainstay of the new, more settled way of life. The introduction of cattle is a clear marker for the Neolithic, and the spread of this new way of life from the Aegean through Central Europe is reflected in the rise in frequency of cattle bones in archaeological assemblages along the way.[2] Whereas it is impossible to be certain whether the earliest Mesolithic inhabitants arrived overland or by sea, there was no land bridge available to the first farmers, and so the domesticated animals, cereal seed and tools that were characteristic of the new way of life had to arrive by sea. It now seems clear, however, that contrary to earlier theories of large-scale migration of people, the new way of life was adopted by the existing Mesolithic population following exposure to farming methods in the normal course of social, domestic and trading life.[3]

The clearance of patches of forest or woodland to make way for cereal planting and herding of domestic animals was a characteristic feature of the introduction of farming. The Burren uplands were particularly attractive in this regard to the earliest farmers. It always seems puzzling from our 21st-century perspective how the apparently barren Burren uplands could have supported a large, thriving and settled farming population. We need to bear a few things in mind when we consider this question:

- Temperatures were higher than they are today, possibly by as much as 1–2 degrees. The uplands did not appear then as they do now, but were covered with pine and hazel woodland. This woodland was easier to clear than the dense, deep-rooted elm and oak forests of lowland regions. At this latitude, a 1 degree rise in temperature also has the effect of extending the grass-growing season by about a month, and so the first farmers were able to maintain their herds on year-round pasture with no need to plan for winter housing or fodder. Consequent year-round natural manuring further improved the soil. Though there may have been outcrops of bare limestone, the soil cover was extensive and fertile enough to support grazing and cereal production in cleared areas. In many places in the Burren today, there are patches of deep, fertile soil that support lush herbs and grasses. They are referred to in Irish as *gáirdíní* [gorjeeny] (little gardens), a name that attests to their importance to our forebears as agricultural resources.

- In contrast to the Mesolithic period, sea levels at the dawn of the Neolithic may have been 4–6 m higher than today, making coastal sections of the Burren uninhabitable.

- At least some of the earliest farmers were semi-nomadic. Having initially cleared sufficient space for grazing and cereal production, they farmed the land for a few generations until the natural fertility of the soil was exhausted and then moved on to clear new areas of woodland and start the cycle again. This pattern is confirmed in pollen records all over Europe, where tree pollen is overtaken by grass, cereal and weed pollen, only to be re-established with subsequent regeneration of cleared woodland. On the other hand, there is widespread evidence in Ireland for permanent settlement, extensive clearance of forest and long-term arable and pastoral farming. In particular, the Céide [kay jeh] Fields in County Mayo provide evidence for a highly organised, settled community that planned and executed the clearance of up to 1,000 hectares of forest and the construction of a linear, enclosed field system during a period of about 500 years between 3700–3200 BC.[4]

Typically, archaeological evidence for the earliest permanent settlements in Ireland dates to the Later Neolithic. In the Burren, however, there is tantalising evidence that might point to a large, active farming community very early in the period. All across the Burren uplands, there are traces of ancient field walls that appear today only as low mounds snaking across the landscape. If you have access to mapping software such as Google Earth or Ordnance Survey Ireland aerial photographs, you can see these field walls. Centre the view on GPS: 52° 59' 15" N, 9° 06' 32" W (GR: R 2555 9355), for example. At an elevation of about 500 m you can clearly make out the patterns made on the landscape by these walls, many of which date to the Neolithic.

Though the field systems of the Burren were quite different to those at the Céide Fields, they indicate a similarly organised, permanent community living in the area from early in the Neolithic. A common characteristic of the Burren and the Céide Fields is a concentration of contemporary megalithic tombs. Portal and court tombs have both been associated with expanding communities, consequent pressure on land and a perceived need to consolidate and define territory. By association and extrapolation from excavated settlements, it appears that some of the ancient field walls of the Burren may date to the Early Neolithic, and may even be contemporary with a chambered tomb (a local type of court tomb) on Roughan Hill dated to 3500–3000 BC.[5] If this is true, then they provide evidence for some of the earliest farming of the Burren uplands. Though contemporary with the Céide Fields, the different form of the field walls and burial monuments indicates that Early Neolithic society was fragmented, and that the earliest Burren farmers adapted to local circumstances in their own distinctive way.[6] They may well be the same people who built the portal tomb at Poulnabrone (7.5 km northwest of Roughan Hill), where ritual deposits of human bones were made around 3200 BC.

Neolithic portal tomb at Poulnabrone (dating to about 3200 BC)

Bronze Age (2400–600 BC)

Neolithic society was probably still quite insular at the end of the period, structured as it was around the needs of large, but localised communities. The Bronze Age, in contrast, saw the beginnings of consolidation, as communities expanded their contact networks and influence, accumulated wealth and established control over large territories. It is becoming clearer that very extensive maritime trade networks were established (or possibly simply expanded), and that many of the cultural changes that characterised the transition to the Bronze Age were introduced by means of these trading networks. A second contributing factor, and one that is directly relevant to the Burren, is a dramatic change in climate that occurred towards the end of the third millennium BC. Evidence from tree rings and pollen analysis shows that the climate cooled and got much wetter around this time. Many of the nutrients in the soil were leached by heavy rainfall, especially on the uplands where forest and woodland had been cleared. There is evidence that much of the soil cover on the Burren uplands was removed by the Middle or Late Bronze Age.[7] Vast areas of the country that had previously been grassland began to be covered by blanket bog due to saturation of the land.

What caused the dramatic change in climate at this time? It is difficult to be certain, but it is probably more than a coincidence that there was a massive volcanic eruption (Hekla 4), dated to about 2300 BC, in Iceland.[8] It is believed that the ash released into the atmosphere by this eruption contributed, at least to some degree, to the ending of the warm period that characterised the Neolithic. As well as darkening the skies and contributing to the onset of a much wetter climate, it is estimated that Hekla 4 dumped about 2 tons of ash per acre in Ireland.[9] Whatever the cause, the effects of the change in climate were profound:

- The land available for agriculture was reduced, putting pressure on population.

- Control of resources became important, and warfare was one of the striking responses to this.

- The Burren uplands were largely depopulated by the end of the Bronze Age. Indeed, the Burren as a whole was marginalised in favour of the power centres in Mooghaun, near Newmarket-on-Fergus, and on the Aran Islands. Depopulation of the Burren is confirmed by a gap in the construction of field walls. Following an initial burst of construction in the Neolithic/Early Bronze Age, the next phase does not begin until the Early Christian Period. This abandonment of the uplands is mirrored by a similar pattern in Britain.[10]

One of the classic markers for the Age that dawned around 2400 BC is a new style of pottery known as Beaker ware, and in the past its appearance was associated with the arrival, en masse, of a new ethnic grouping that came to be known as Beaker Folk. An 'invasion' now seems unlikely, but the sheer range of 'cultural' and material innovations from this time is striking, and it is hard to believe that they all occurred spontaneously within the native population. Beaker pottery is known from all over Central and Western Europe, and it appears to have developed and spread in a relatively short space of time. Some was traded, although a number of Irish examples were manufactured locally. Some was decorative, but other pieces appear to have been functional. Much of the surviving pottery is associated with new types of burial ritual, occasionally involving single, crouched burials. Skeletal remains found in Beaker burials in Britain point to an intriguing aspect of the spread of Beaker pottery; it often corresponds with the spread of a different skull shape – broader than that found in earlier burials. The significance of this association is debated, and it is by no means certain that the invasion model is valid. However, there can be no doubt that there was considerable movement of people throughout Europe at this time, both transitory in the form of traders and more permanent in the form of immigrants. Many of the broad skulled remains are of apparently isolated females, possibly indicating that it was not uncommon for traders to return to Britain and Ireland with continental 'wives'.

Beaker pottery has been found in the Burren at a farmstead on Roughan Hill excavated by Dr Carleton Jones. The discovery of hundreds of sherds of pottery was important in allowing him to date the farmstead to the transition from Neolithic to Bronze Age, and indeed a single sherd of a (probably later) type of pottery points to continued occupation into the Early Bronze Age.

Notwithstanding the farmstead on Roughan Hill, there is a scarcity of evidence for settlement structures in the Burren in the earliest part of the Bronze Age; this is not surprising, as it is true also of the rest of Ireland and of Europe as a whole. It may be because any structures that were used were lightly built, possibly of timber, and have simply not survived, but it is also probably due to the fact that Bronze Age settlers seem for the most part to have preferred low-lying areas. This is not to say that they never built on high ground – the massive enclosure at Mooghaun, and possibly also that on Turlough Hill, date to the Bronze Age. In general, however, the scarcity of Bronze Age settlement evidence in the Burren is probably accounted for by depopulation of the uplands in favour of low-lying sites.

Although there were horses in Ireland before the last Ice Age, there is no clear evidence for native wild horses between the end of the last Ice Age and the beginning of the Bronze Age, when they show up again in the record.[11] Horses must, therefore, have been reintroduced to Ireland around this time.

A new type of barbed and tanged arrowhead also makes its first appearance around this time, as does a previously unknown accessory, a wristguard used by archers to protect the wrist from the lash of the bowstring.

A further innovation of the period was the use of copper. Probably introduced slightly later than the first Beaker pottery, the means of introduction and spread is unclear. There is a possibility that, following introduction from Iberia or Central Europe, an indigenous metalworking industry developed. After millennia of stoneworking, Neolithic people knew their rocks and could not have been unaware of the characteristics and properties of the different types available to them. It may have taken no more than a hint from outside to point them in the direction of the abundant copper ore to be found in the south of the country. It is even possible that a copper industry developed spontaneously in Kerry, where a mine at Ross Island near Killarney is the earliest known copper mine in Western Europe. A copper axehead found near Lake Inchiquin on the southern boundary of the Burren dates to the earliest stages of the Bronze Age.

The logical progression from copper-working is the production of bronze (an alloy of copper and tin), but this presents a problem in the Irish context; namely, the apparent scarcity of native tin. It is not unknown in the country – there are sources in Wicklow, for example – but there does not appear to have been enough to support a bronze-working industry of the scale that existed in Ireland at the time.[12] So where did the Irish metalworkers get their tin? Once again, it is hard to escape the conclusion that there was a lot of trading going on in the Bronze Age, and that the west coast of Ireland, including the Aran Islands, was an important element in an extensive trading network. By the Late Bronze Age, bronze swords, spearheads, bracelets and pins were being manufactured at Dun Aonghusa on Inis Mór.

Society seems to have become much more hierarchical over the course of the Bronze Age. As with the transition from the Mesolithic to the Neolithic, the physical differences that separated the Neolithic and Bronze Ages – in materials, tools, structures, burials etc. – were accompanied by changes at the conceptual level. It might be stretching the imagination too much to say that it was the first capitalist society, but trade, division of labour and the accumulation of wealth do seem to have been important!

What triggered people to move from an apparently egalitarian society to one where control of trade and availability of cheap labour provided by those of lower rank were important? Archaeological evidence in the form of weaponry, exotic imported materials and personal ornamentation points to a society with a 'warrior elite' at the top rank and one or more lower orders providing labour for mundane tasks such as construction and farming. Why were finely worked personal gold ornaments such as bracelets, torcs and earrings important if not to show that their wearers were people of high status? Archaeology has uncovered and interpreted the physical evidence, but the reasons for stratification of society probably have more to do with psychology. People finally conceptualised the unholy trinity of wealth, power and influence.

Although no direct evidence of goldworking has been found in the Burren, one of the most beautiful and intricately worked gold objects of the Late Bronze Age was found in a gryke in the Burren limestone in 1932. The Gleninsheen Gorget, now in the care of the National Museum of Ireland, is a very finely worked gold collar ornament that can hardly have had any use other than as an ostentatious display of wealth and status.

The so-called 'Mooghaun Hoard' of gold objects, discovered in 1854 but now mostly lost, is the largest such hoard ever found in Europe, and in conjunction with other gold objects found in the area provides evidence for a highly structured society in the Late Bronze Age. The practical application of accumulated wealth in the Bronze Age is not fully understood. Valuable objects were almost certainly traded or exchanged. But the Mooghaun Hoard demonstrates an important aspect of Bronze Age society that is repeated elsewhere – ritual deposition of valuable objects. 'In bullion terms alone this hoard represents an enormous resource which it seems the local community was prepared to offer or sacrifice by its ritual abandonment in what must have been regarded as a sacred place.'[13]

Recent research suggests that much of the gold used in the manufacture of personal ornaments such as the Gleninsheen Gorget and the objects from the Mooghaun Hoard came from the Mourne Mountains in County Down, indicating mobility in Bronze Age society and the existence of a well-established trading and manufacturing infrastructure.[14]

One of the most characteristic Bronze Age monuments known today was not recognised as such until relatively recently. *Fulacht Fiadh* [fullokth feeah] is the term used to describe a low, usually horseshoe-shaped mound of burnt stones with a pit or trough at the centre. Pits were normally dug at the water table so that they would fill naturally with water and avoid leakage. Occasionally, however, they seem to have been dug near streams and may have had to be filled manually. The term was used originally in ninth-century Irish literature to describe open-air cooking places used by roving bands of warriors known as *fianna* [feeanna]. A *fulacht* is a cooking place, and *fiadh* may refer to these warrior bands, the deer cooked in the pits or simply the wilderness in which these cooking places are often found. In any event, it is unfortunate that the term has been used to describe this type of monument as the cooking places of the *fianna* referred to in the literature post-date by up to 2,000 years the mounds now known as *fulachta fiadh* (*fulachta* is the plural). Archaeologists today tend to use the neutral term 'burnt mound' to describe these monuments, and there may be as many as 45,000 in the country.[15] It is by no means certain that they were cooking places, although experiment has demonstrated that large joints of meat can successfully be boiled in the pits. They may have been used as 'sweathouses', for bathing, for dyeing cloth, in the preparation of leather, or simply some other function that has been obscured with the passage of time. About 300 *fulachta fiadh* have

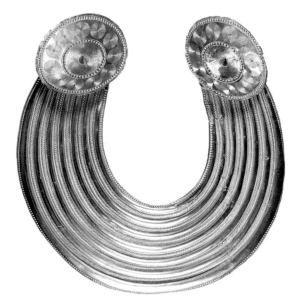

The Gleninsheen Gorget, Late Bronze Age, 800–700 BC
(courtesy National Museum of Ireland)

been identified in County Clare, with concentrations in the eastern part of the Burren and on the waterways north and east of Ennis.

The wedge tomb is the latest in the sequence of megalithic burial monuments, dating to the transition from Neolithic to Bronze Age. Earlier monument types were court, portal and passage tombs. One of the densest concentrations of wedge tombs in the country is found in the Burren. These are low, usually wedge-shaped burial chambers with the wide end consistently oriented towards the west or southwest. They date generally to the second half of the third millennium BC (c. 2500–2000 BC), and it is remarkable to think that these monuments were being built by Bronze Age people living in the Burren at the same time that the great pyramids were being built in Egypt!

Iron Age (600 BC–AD 400)

Though there is plenty of archaeological evidence dating to the Neolithic all over the Burren, we have seen that much less remains from the Bronze Age. Unfortunately, this trend continues into the Iron Age, and we are left to speculate to an even greater degree about the type of society that might have been characteristic of the period. Until relatively recently, this gap in our knowledge was padded out by the 'Celtic' mythology, whereby Ireland was believed to have been invaded by a fierce, warlike army speaking a new exotic language, bringing with it a rich heritage of art and folklore and providing the bloodline from which the true, 'Gaelic' Irish descended.

There may well have been an influx of new people into Ireland, possibly over a long period. There are accounts of whole tribes wandering around Europe from around the middle of the fifth century BC following a period of turmoil. Some of these mass movements resulted in violence, for example in Italy and Greece. But Ireland, during the earliest part of what is known as the Iron Age, seems to have suffered an 'uncharacteristic insular isolation', and the period from 600–300 BC is very obscure.[16]

Time and patient archaeological and linguistic investigation will help to clarify the picture, but there is already enough evidence to suggest that the new 'culture' became established in the same way as its Bronze Age and Neolithic predecessors – slowly, and facilitated by trading and social contacts along the maritime trading routes of the Atlantic seaboard and the Irish Sea.

Iron, like bronze, was used in Europe for some time before it reached Ireland. The two metals were actually used contemporaneously, with iron often used simply to imitate bronze objects such as socketed axes and sickles and, by the end of the Bronze Age, iron rivets occasionally used to repair bronze cauldrons. The scarcity of iron objects in the archaeological record is due in part to the fact that it is subject to rust and less durable than bronze. Nonetheless, there are sufficient similarities among surviving objects of various types discovered across Ireland, Britain and parts of Europe to suggest that there was (notwithstanding the possible hiatus between 600–300 BC) considerable back-and-forth movement of material and of people throughout both Bronze and Iron Ages. These movements of people, and associated developments in technology, materials, artistic styles and indeed language, should probably be seen as elements of social and trading networks, and not as the warlike invasion that has been proposed in the past as the trigger for the 'Celticisation' of Ireland. Such an invasion would imply a one-way, large-scale, sudden movement of people, bringing with them and imposing on the indigenous population a radically different culture. There is simply not enough evidence to support this scenario. Rather, the Irish were playing their part in the broadly defined culture that spanned the whole of Western and Central Europe, not only as recipients of new influences, but also as innovators in their own right.

Horse trappings, usually of bronze, form a large proportion of the Iron Age objects found in Ireland, and three pieces bear witness to the use of horses in the Burren at the time. Two horsebits, one of which was discarded some time after it was identified, were found near Corrofin. The third piece, found at Ballyalla, near Kilshanny, is known as a 'bridle pendant', a type of object that has not been found anywhere outside Ireland. The function of these objects is unclear, but it appears likely that they were used to lead horses on foot rather than by reins.

As already noted, it is almost impossible, given the scarcity of evidence, to reconstruct a comprehensive social and economic picture of the Iron Age. We have almost no idea of how or where the ordinary people lived. We can only speculate that they might have lived in round timber huts, based on the remains of apparently ceremonial structures of the period. It has even been suggested that some, at least, may have lived in tents, and this suggestion seems as plausible as any other.[17]

Early Medieval/Early Christian (AD 400–1169)

After the archaeological desert of the Iron Age, it is a relief to witness an explosion of archaeological remains during the Early Medieval period. This is the age of ringforts, crannógs, early churches and monasteries, superb gold-work, illustrated texts … and the Vikings! The Burren experienced a revival during this period, and there is evidence everywhere of settlement and worship, farming and feuding, fact and folklore.

We cannot adequately understand the period without first considering the contemporary relationship between the spiritual and the secular. During the Iron Age, little or no distinction was made between the secular, physical world on the one hand and the spiritual or mythical world on the other. The coming of Christianity did little to change this 'pagan' world view for at least the first two centuries of the Early Medieval period. The keepers of the spiritual flame, whether you call them druids, high priests, abbots or bishops, were powerful people and were accorded places of honour in society. Pagan practices were assimilated into the Irish Christian tradition to such an extent that it is often hard to distinguish between the two. Many of the 'holy wells' in the Burren and throughout the country, for example, had their origins in pre-Christian ritual and belief.

Ireland was unusual in Western Europe in that it was never subject to the organisational discipline of Rome, whose armies exercised control from North Africa to southern Scotland. In those areas controlled by Rome, the Church was organised into dioceses, centred on the great cities and towns and controlled by bishops. Christianity was recognised by Constantine the Great in AD 313 as the official state religion of the Roman Empire. The Edict of Milan in that year ended (temporarily, as it turned out) the oppression of Christians and it was only then that they were able to expand more or less unhindered across the Empire. Contrary to popular opinion, however, St Patrick was not sent by Rome to convert the pagan Irish to Christianity. In fact, he was not even the first Christian in Ireland; there was a Christian community here by the time Palladius was sent from Gaul in AD 431 to administer to 'the Irish believing in Christ'. This is an intriguing aspect of the development of the early Irish church that, for want of evidence, has not yet been told. Who were the earliest Christians in Ireland? How and why did they come here? The possibility that they were more aligned with the Orthodox Christian traditions of Egypt than with the now more familiar Roman version of Christianity cannot be ruled out. Future lines of investigation into the story of the arrival of Christianity in Ireland should take account of the strong evidence of an early eremitic tradition in Ireland, familiarity with events in the eastern Mediterranean among early Irish chroniclers and the fascinating recovery in 2006 of an eighth-century manuscript called 'The Faddan More Psalter'. The Coptic-style satchel that protected the psalter (prayer book) was lined with Egyptian papyrus – the only example of this material ever found in Ireland.

By the time Palladius arrived in Ireland, there had already been considerable contact with the Roman Empire in Gaul and especially in Britain. A number of gold and silver hoards found here may have been 'spoils of war' brought back from northern Britain and Wales by Irish raiding parties. St Patrick himself was first brought to Ireland as a slave by one of these raiding parties. Though Ireland was never invaded by the Romans, a military expedition was considered in the first century AD by Agricola, who saw merit in using Ireland to connect Britain and Spain. Ireland's ports and harbours were better known to the Romans than those of Britain: 'We know most of its harbours and approaches, and that through the intercourse of commerce.'[18] There is other evidence for trading links with Roman Britain, possibly including a trading post of some sort at Drumanagh in north County Dublin.

This was the context for the early development of the church in Ireland. A fragmented and rural society, whose chieftains were accustomed to wielding power and influence over large areas and whose high priests enjoyed privileged status, was unlikely to submit to a new order introduced from outside. Indeed, Palladius couldn't wait to get out of the country, having received a generally hostile reception.[19] Nevertheless, the early Christians persisted and an organisation of sorts, administered by bishops, was established. But to use modern terminology, the Irish church was at the end of the supply-chain; without the support and organisational resources of Rome, it was more or less left to develop in its own unique way. The intimate relationships between secular and spiritual developed with the times (albeit with the integration of an episcopal layer) and the organisation of the early church seems to have mirrored that of secular society. Throughout the Early Medieval period, the two were intertwined in a way not seen in areas where Roman influence was dominant. Bishoprics and monastic settlements existed side by side, but the latter were patronised and populated by powerful families and were the principal organisational structure. The abbot was appointed by the chieftain, and the position of abbot was often hereditary as it was not unknown for abbots to be married. It was not until the end of the Early Medieval period in the twelfth century that the Irish church returned to the fold with the restoration of episcopal hierarchy and formalisation of the monastic sector on continental lines. Even then, however, as we shall see, the Irish could not resist the temptation to bend the rules. Examples of their impertinence are to be found in the Burren!

We know much more about the social and political organisation of the Early Medieval period because by this time writing had been introduced to Ireland. The earliest form of writing was Ogham, a script based on Latin with an alphabet consisting of twenty characters, with five later additions. Ogham probably developed during the fourth century and continued in use until the seventh or eighth century, but it was unwieldy and not suitable for narrative writing.[20] There is, however, a rich tradition of manuscript writing from the period, and much of it has been valuable in shedding light on historical events, personalities and society.

The wealthier landowning class settled predominantly in family groups in ringforts, and these are the most common archaeological monuments from this period. At least 45,000 have been recorded throughout the country, with up to 500 in the Burren. Various forms of ringfort were used, from very small enclosures with a single bank and ditch to large, two- or three-ring examples, and from simple earthen structures to elaborate stone forts with massive defensive walls. The stone version is more common in the west of Ireland, presumably because stone is in plentiful supply. This is especially so in the Burren where there are over 300 stone forts, also known as cashels or cahers. For the visitor to the Burren, an interesting comparison can be made by visiting two monuments within 1 km of each other on the road (R480) between Ballyvaghan and Leamaneh Castle. The Rath (GR: M 2242 0499) is a large earthen ringfort typical of its type. In use, its high earthen bank was topped by a palisade fence to help keep animals in and rustlers out. Caher Mór (GR: M 2199 0447) is a cashel or stone fort that, though modified in the fifteenth century, shows clearly the different form of construction used for this type of ringfort. Souterrains – from the French *sous* (under) and *terrain* (ground) – are often associated with ringforts. These are short underground passages that may have been used as places of refuge or for safe keeping of valuables in time of conflict, or they may have been used simply for storage of perishable food.

There is some debate regarding the dating of ringforts, and evidence is coming to light of settlement in ringforts in the Iron Age. Certainly, they were an important form of settlement from about the fifth century, flourishing between the seventh and ninth centuries, but the extent of construction from the tenth century onwards is not completely clear. Two factors contributed to the development of alternative settlement patterns:

• Though large communities had grown up around the principal monastic centres such as Armagh and Clonmacnois, the first purpose-built secular urban settlements in Ireland were the *longphuirt* [lungfuirth] or ports established by the Vikings, possibly as early as the mid-ninth century.

• The arrival of the Anglo-Normans in AD 1169 saw the expansion of the Viking towns and the establishment of chartered settlements or villages throughout much of Ireland.

Nevertheless, it appears that some ringforts continued to be occupied at least until the seventeenth century, mostly in those parts of the country where the Anglo-Norman influence was not so strong. The Burren, situated as it was outside the direct sphere of Anglo-Norman influence, and with an abundance of building material in the form of limestone slabs, was one of those areas where ringforts continued in use for a long period. One of the best preserved of these cashels is Cahermacnaghten. The cashel itself is but one element of an extensive settlement that included the law school of the O'Davoren family, traditionally the legal advisors to the O'Loughlins, who were a dominant Gaelic chiefdom in the area from the end of the Early Medieval period.

A cashel at Ballykinvarga (2 km northeast of Kilfenora) is enigmatic,

Caher Mór – remains of the fifteenth-century gatehouse

and highlights one of the unsolved riddles of the period. It is one of only four forts in Ireland to include a *chevaux de frise* in its defences. *Chevaux de frise* is a modern name for bands of stone slabs set on end around habitation sites as a means of impeding the progress of attackers. (The term means 'Frisian horses' and dates to the Medieval period when it referred to portable defensive obstacles used against advancing cavalry.) Although a number of sites in Britain included *chevaux de frise,* the greatest concentration is in Iberia, reinforcing suggestions of ongoing links between this region and Ireland. An alternative suggestion is that wooden *chevaux de frise* were common throughout Europe and that what we can see today are nothing more than the stone survivors of a widespread feature of Iron Age defended sites. It may simply be that the *chevaux de frise* at Ballykinvarga was an experimental construction in stone of a more common wooden defensive feature.

In the Early Medieval period, interminable power struggles resulted in a territorial division based on family groups. Among the principal families in the Burren at the end of the Early Medieval period were the O'Loughlins and the O'Connors; the records show various members of both families having control over the area at different times from the beginning of the eleventh century. At that time, the area was known as *Corcu Modruadh* [kurku mruah], a reference to a previously predominant grouping. This is the origin of the anglicised name of Corcomroe and corresponds almost exactly with the area now known as the Burren.

Into this fluid mix towards the end of the first millennium AD, came the expansionist *Dál gCais* [dhawl gash] group, at that time an insignificant sept but the ultimate forerunners of the O'Brien family who came to

Cahermacnaghten – ancestral residence of the O'Davoren brehons

Cahercommaun outer walls

dominate the area during the Medieval period. As we shall see, the early part of the Medieval period in the Burren is dominated by constant jockeying for position and influence among these groups.

Some of the finest examples of early Irish art date to the Early Medieval period. It is the age of illuminated manuscripts such as the Book of Kells and of elaborate metalwork such as the Ardagh Chalice and the Cross of Cong. Most of the surviving artwork is ecclesiastical and much of it is connected with pilgrimage, a practice that was common throughout Europe at the time and that continues to this day. There is plenty of evidence to suggest that pilgrimage was common in the Burren, but little remains of the associated artwork.

While much Irish artwork of the time (particularly precious metal pieces) appears to have fallen into the hands of Viking raiding parties, it seems unlikely that the Vikings can be blamed for the scarcity of artwork in the Burren. They established a settlement in Limerick, but their influence does not appear to have extended much beyond the settlement and there is scant evidence of Viking activity in the Burren. What influence they did have appears, on present evidence at least, to have been concentrated in the area of Cahercommaun. An iron arrowhead recovered during excavation of the cashel is Scandinavian, and a very fine Viking necklace discovered recently during excavation at Glencurran Cave near Cahercommaun is the largest ever found in Ireland. The necklace includes a number of large hollow beads that are very rare and not usually found outside Scandinavia. It is provisionally dated to AD 820–850 and was probably originally manufactured in Norway or Sweden.[21]

We should not leave the Early Medieval period without mentioning the unique legal code that was used in Ireland at the time. Developing possibly since the Iron Age in the oral tradition, Brehon Law became codified in the seventh century and is now regarded as having been very progressive. The focus was on restitution rather than punishment and detention of wrongdoers. Crimes and misdemeanours and the level of restitution required to compensate victims of each were described in minute detail. There was admirable concern for the environment; women and men, though in many cases dealt with separately, were afforded comparable protection; contracts were sacred; there was no death penalty in law, though murderers could be handed over to victims' families to face extrajudicial revenge; different ranks in society were defined and regulated. The whole body of Brehon Law was complex, written in archaic terms (probably reflecting its antiquity) and extremely detailed.

Consequently, it needed to be interpreted by highly trained scholars. These were the brehons, and they were more like modern university professors than judges. Their function was to interpret the code and describe the rules to concerned parties rather than to hand down judgements and establish precedent in the way modern courts do. Brehon Law continued in use in the Early Medieval period throughout Ireland, and into the Medieval in those areas of the country where the Anglo-Norman and English influence was weak. There were at least two – possibly three – Brehon law schools in the Burren: the O'Davorens, who were lawyers to the O'Loughlin family, had their school near Cahermacnaghten; the Mc Clancy school at Knockfin near Doolin interpreted the law on behalf of the O'Briens; and the O'Dalys, who had a bardic school at Finavarra, may also have been brehons to a branch of the O'Loughlins. Brehon Law went into terminal decline in the Burren in the sixteenth century when some of the principal families submitted to the Crown. It was finally abolished when James I became King of England in 1603.

Medieval (AD 1169–c. 1530)

The arrival of the Anglo-Normans in 1169 is traditionally used to define the end of the Early Medieval and the beginning of the Medieval in Ireland. Though the physical imprints of their arrival (new villages and towns, and the large castles built as centres of administration) were confined in the early years of the new era to the eastern half of the country, the social and political effects were felt countrywide almost immediately. To understand this, it is useful to view the Anglo-Normans as merely another faction in the mosaic of alliances and rivalries that characterised contemporary society in Ireland. For centuries beforehand, the country had witnessed almost unending feuding among the powerful clans. In the Burren, for example, the fortunes of the *Corcu Modruadh*, the *Uí Fidgeinti* [ee fine-tee], the *Dál gCais* and others had ebbed and flowed as alliances were formed and dissolved and as each grouping attempted to gain advantage for itself. The powerful Medieval Gaelic lordships began to take shape towards the end of the Early Medieval period, and in the west of Ireland the O'Briens of Thomond jockeyed constantly for position with the O'Connors of Connaught.

In another theatre, this time in the southeast of the country, the assistance Dermot Mac Murrough received from King Henry II, albeit by proxy in the person of Strongbow, could be viewed as nothing more than an unusually enterprising example of such an alliance. The direct cause of the underlying feud was, after all, a local matter; Mac Murrough had abducted his rival Tiernan O'Rourke's wife in 1152! Fourteen years later, as O'Rourke was about to exact revenge, Mac Murrough fled the country in search of military assistance, and the rest, as the saying goes, is history.

Some of the earliest archaeological evidence of the new era comes from County Wexford, where one of the first groups of Anglo-Normans landed at Baginbun and built a fortified enclosure not unlike the native promontory forts. Later archaeological remains throughout the country trace the development of Anglo-Norman defended structures through motte-and-bailey, ringwork and various types of castle through to the ubiquitous tower houses of the fifteenth to seventeenth centuries. Though no stone castles were built in the Burren, there are many examples of the later tower houses. These, however, were built by the Gaelic lords of the area, the O'Loughlins, O'Connors and O'Briens, for example, rather than by Anglo-Normans.

The momentous changes of the twelfth and thirteenth centuries were not confined to the secular sphere, and the archaeological evidence traces the assimilation of the old semi-independent Irish church into the mainstream of Christianity. To what extent the Anglo-Normans were responsible for these changes is debatable; much of the institutional reform had begun by the time they arrived. The new, Romanesque style of architecture, for example, had been introduced in 1127 with the construction of Cormac's Chapel on the Rock of Cashel. The established continental monastic orders were introduced in 1142 when the Cistercians built their first Irish abbey at Mellifont. There can be no doubt that the Anglo-Norman penchant for organisation and centralised administration facilitated the transformation of the Irish church, but nothing, it seems, could quite eliminate the quirky Irish imprint that had been a feature of the previous centuries.

This imprint is clearly visible at a number of ecclesiastical monuments in the Burren. Elements of the Gothic architectural style favoured by the Anglo-Normans were borrowed and combined with the existing Romanesque in a transitional style known as the 'School of the West'. Corcomroe Abbey and Kilfenora Cathedral include some of the best examples of this transitional style in the country. Some of the features at Corcomroe in particular also demonstrate that (a) some contemporary Irish architects would have benefited from formal training in their craft and (b) Irish masons were not averse to bending the rules when it suited them!

The bishops themselves, who had been superimposed on the old monastic establishment in an attempt to bring the Irish church to order, continued to dabble in secular affairs. So little regard had some for their religious responsibilities that a historian of the Diocese of Killaloe felt compelled to describe the most blatant offenders thus: 'But as for their being bishops, this was a mere colourable pretext, the better to engraft religious war upon hostility of races, and thereby promote at once ecclesiastical revenge and imperial ambition.'[22]

By the beginning of the fourteenth century the old chiefdom of Corcomroe had been consolidated as a semi-political entity, and it corresponded with the Diocese of Kilfenora, established in 1152. Political control of the region was far from clear, however. As we have seen, control transferred many times between the O'Connors and O'Loughlins, but eventually the territory was divided into two civil divisions known as baronies. The western portion became the Barony of Corcomroe, and for the first time the term Burren came formally into general use with the establishment of the Barony of Burren in the east.

The 'transitional style' of architecture

Corcomroe Abbey –
east window
(courtesy Mark Carthy)

Corcomroe Abbey –
south transept and nave
(courtesy Mark Carthy)

Kilfenora Cathedral –
east window
(courtesy Mark Carthy)

Corcomroe Abbey – thirteenth-century Cistercian monastery (courtesy Mark Carthy)

The widespread socio-economic decline of the fourteenth century is recorded at Corcomroe Abbey. Evidence from this monument shows clearly that the Burren suffered as much as any other region in the country from the effects of the Great European Famine of 1315–17 and the Black Death of 1348–50, not to mention the continuing in-fighting among the Gaelic chiefdoms. The decline of Corcomroe Abbey also heralds a hiatus in the archaeological record that continued until conditions improved and the great chiefdoms of O'Brien and O'Loughlin were able to consolidate their positions and bring some sort of order to the Burren. The following 200 years (c. 1450–1650) saw the construction of all the Burren tower houses, the ruins of which can be seen throughout the area today.

Ecclesiastical Monuments

Before we begin the detailed description of the monuments, a few words relating specifically to ecclesiastical monuments are appropriate.

The great variety of ecclesiastical monuments to be found all over the Burren is testament to the importance of the area during Early Medieval and Medieval times, and also to the pervasive influence of a peculiarly Irish version of Christianity that developed during the Early Medieval period. The Burren is exceptional in the sheer number of such monuments: two Burren parishes include nine ecclesiastical monuments and others are almost as well endowed whereas most parishes in Ireland have just one, two or occasionally three ecclesiastical monuments.[23] These figures exclude the dozens of isolated holy wells scattered throughout the area. Ecclesiastical monuments range from simple holy wells through the most primitive single-cell early Christian churches to an elaborate and very interesting Cistercian abbey.

Ecclesiastical monuments are always associated with one or more of the following features, examples of many of which can be found in the Burren:

- **Vallum** – A wall or bank that delineates the sacred part of the site. Examples in the Burren include monuments at Oughtmama, Corcomroe and Templecronan.

- **Church** – The earliest churches were timber structures and there is no documentary evidence for stone churches before the late seventh century.[24] No timber church has yet been identified in the Burren, but it is almost certain that some of the earliest stone churches replaced earlier timber versions.

- **Burial Ground/Cemetery** – The earliest burial grounds may only be identified by the presence of simple stone markers, but many have been reused or have continued in use through the Christian period. Many of the cemeteries in the Burren include simple stone grave markers.

- **Founder's Tomb/Shrine** – Generally located very close to the church, these are often tent-shaped stone structures that originally contained either the remains of, or something belonging to, the founder of the site. They were important focal points for pilgrimage. The best examples in the Burren are found at Templecronan.

- **Cross-Inscribed Stone** – There is considerable overlap in the Early Christian period between pagan and Christian practice, and many pre-Christian standing stones were reused as markers for Christian worship. Later cross-inscribed stones are purely Christian.

- **High Cross** – The development of the so-called Celtic high cross can be traced back to the earliest cross inscribed stones. Decoration on some of the more elaborate surviving crosses suggests that there may have been early wooden examples. In many cases, high crosses were not intended as representations of the crucifixion, but illustrated scenes from scripture to a largely illiterate people. They were also used occasionally to make 'political' statements or to commemorate events or people. They do not appear to have been used as grave markers. Kilfenora is known as 'The City of the Crosses' and a number of fine examples can be found there.

- **Sundial** – Sundials, though uncommon, are believed to have been used to mark out monastic daily routine, with the rays of the dial defining the formal periods of community prayer that were so much a part of monastic life. No examples are known from the Burren.

- **Round Tower** – Traditionally viewed as refuges from pillaging Vikings, it is now believed that this was not the primary function of round towers. Defence was certainly a consideration in their construction as most of the entrances were built above ground level and were accessible only by means of a wooden ladder that could be withdrawn in time of danger. However, this provided scant defence. Their 3–8 storeys were divided by timber floors and there are records of round towers having been burnt by Viking raiders. Known in the Irish language as *cloigteach* [klig-chock], meaning bell-house, they were used as bell towers (for hand-held bells) and possibly as markers for pilgrims. The defensive element in their construction was probably for protection of the community's ecclesiastical valuables such as chalices, silver plate, precious manuscripts etc. Round towers are usually to be found to the northwest or southwest of the church, with their entrances facing the entrance of the church. The remains of a round tower can be seen at the church in Killinaboy, while one of the tallest examples in the country can be found at Kilmacduagh near Gort.

- **Holy Well** – The origins of holy wells are obscure; many were used in pre-Christian times as foci for ritual activity and were assimilated into the Christian tradition. Spring wells would have been essential sources of fresh water for any settled ecclesiastical community and may have come to be used as gathering places or rest stops for pilgrims. Whatever the origins, they have a long tradition and many remain important pilgrimage sites to this day. There are dozens of holy wells in the Burren, with fine examples at Oughtmama, Gleninagh and St Mac Duagh's Hermitage.

- **Bullaun Stone** – The origins of bullaun stones are equally obscure and it is difficult to separate fact from myth and tradition. They are small boulders with one or more hollows on the upper surface. The hollows may be the result of grinding of cereals for food or other plants for medicinal purposes, in which case the bullauns were simply mortars. They may also have contained water with alleged curative powers – some are associated with cures for warts. There is a bullaun stone in the graveyard at Rathborney church, another at St Mac Duagh's Hermitage and another possible example reused in the jamb of the north door at Killilagh church.

- **Souterrain** – Though often associated with cashels and other forts, these underground chambers or passages are also associated with ecclesiastical sites, for example Rathborney, Crumlin and Oughtdara churches. Their primary function may have been for storage of perishable food, but there are also accounts of their being used for refuge and storage of valuables.

The Burren is intimately associated with a particular type of ecclesiastical object known as a Tau cross. Three examples can be found in the Burren, and another just outside at Dysert O'Dea, a few kilometers southwest of Corrofin. The best known example is the 'Cross of Innawee' or the 'Cross of Killinaboy', which can be seen in the Heritage Centre in Corrofin. It was replaced in its original position at the side of the road between Killinaboy and Leamaneh Castle by a replica, and it has been the subject of much speculation since it was first described in 1808. Shaped like the top of a crutch, this particular example was one of three used to mark the boundary of the termon lands of the monastic settlement at Killinaboy. Also at Killinaboy, there is a carving of a Tau cross on a grave slab in the southeast corner of the graveyard. The Tau cross is also represented on two high crosses – The Doorty Cross at Kilfenora and St Tola's Cross at Dysert O'Dea – where it forms the top section of staffs or croziers carried by two carved ecclesiastical figures. These carvings have also been the subject of much commentary and speculation. The cross at Dysert O'Dea shows two clerics holding a Tau-headed staff between them, with another figure to one side holding a staff or crozier with a crooked head. The carving at Kilfenora shows two clerics with arms linked, one holding a Tau-headed staff and the other holding a crooked staff or crozier. What story are these carvings telling us?

Michael J. C. Buckley, writing in 1900, might have provided part of the answer. Quoting from *Histoire de l'Abbaye de Morimond, par l'Abbé Dubois*, he says that monks took possession of forests and moorlands in the following manner:

> The abbot, holding a wooden crutch or cross staff in his hand went forward in front of the brothers, diggers, or woodcutters, all reciting the Psalms. Having got to the place in the forest, or on the moorland, which had been given to them, the abbot planted his 'cross' staff thereon, sprinkling the spot with holy water all round, and taking possession thereof, in the name of Christ. He then, accompanied by the brethren, went round the territory. If it were a forest, the abbot first cut down a tree; if it were uncultivated land, he dug the first spade of its soil; his brethren immediately followed his example, and thus commenced the first essays of agriculture on a regular system, not only in Ireland, but all through the countries of Europe, even to the confines of Asia.[25]

He goes on to say that on such occasions the bishop of the adjoining territory was present as a witness only to the foundation of the monastery.

The Tau symbol (so called after the T-shaped nineteenth letter of the Greek alphabet) has a long history in Christianity. St Anthony the Great, one of the monastic Desert Fathers in Egypt in the third to fourth centuries is traditionally shown with a T-shaped crutch. It seems likely therefore that these Tau crosses are symbols of the Early Medieval monastic or eremitic tradition that was such an important feature of life in the Burren at the time.

Conclusion

If the foregoing introduction to the archaeology of the Burren has highlighted more questions than answers, it is indicative as much of the current state of Irish archaeological research in general as of our knowledge of the history and prehistory of the Burren in particular. Humans may have been late arriving in Ireland, but since arriving they have left such a volume and variety of monuments and artefacts that archaeologists are condemned to a never-ending game of catch-up. Thankfully, the challenge is being taken up and discoveries are being made every year that are helping to throw new light on the secrets of our past.

Site of 'axe factory' at the mouth of the River Aille in Fisherstreet near Doolin, County Clare.

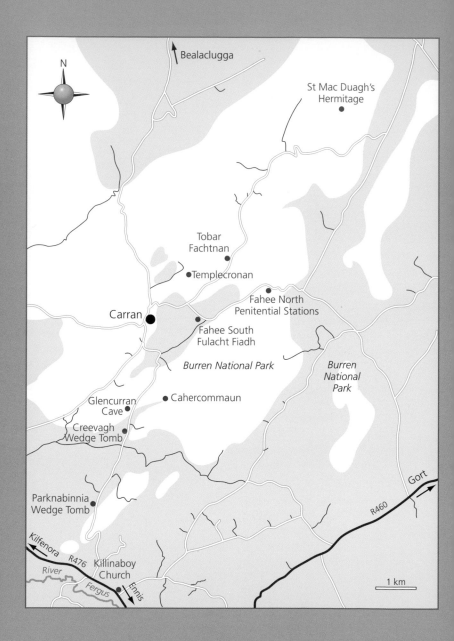

N

Bealaclugga

St Mac Duagh's
Hermitage

Tobar
Fachtnan

Templecronan

Fahee North
Penitential Stations

Carran

Fahee South
Fulacht Fiadh

Burren National Park

*Burren
National
Park*

Cahercommaun

Glencurran
Cave

Creevagh
Wedge Tomb

Parknabinnia
Wedge Tomb

Gort

R460

Kilfenora

R476

Killinaboy
Church

River

Fergus

Ennis

1 km

Burren East

PART 2

Burren East

Killinaboy Church
GR: R 2711 9157

The early history of Killinaboy church is not fully understood; its name *Cill Inghine Bhaoith* [kill ineena vwee] – only contributes to the confusion. The one thing we can say for certain about the name is that it refers to a church – *cill* being the equivalent Irish word. The second part of the name is a combination of two Irish words, *inghine* and *baoith*, and this is where the confusion arises. *Inghine* could be a misspelling of *Finghin* [fineen], an early saint about whom little is known other than that he is the patron saint of an area in east Clare called Quin and of the O'Quin family. It could also be a misspelling of *inÍon* [ineen], the Irish word for daughter. This has led to the suggestion that Killinaboy was founded in the seventh century by St Findclú [finclue], the daughter of Báith [boy] according to an early Irish text.[1] *Ingena,* a Latin word, may have been an early designation for a group of religious women, possibly some sort of convent.

If not Findclú's father, Baoith may have been another equally obscure early saint associated with an old Irish clan called *Clann d'Ifearnáin* [klon differnawn]. This clan's territory was centered on Corrofin in the latter part of the tenth century. *Clann d'Ifearnáin* was a name used to refer to the *Uí Chuinn* [ee kwin] (O'Quin) family, and the circular reference to St Finghin should be obvious. Alternatively, the word *baoith* [bwee] may be an adjective used to describe *inghine,* in which case the confusion is further compounded by the variety of possible translations![2] Three holy wells in the present day Killinaboy parish are also dedicated to Inghine Bhaoith. Further references (direct, circular and tentative) can be found throughout eastern and central County Clare and indeed further afield.

Whatever the origins of the name, we can be certain that a church was established at Killinaboy in the Early Medieval period. That Killinaboy was an early monastic settlement is confirmed by the presence in the church grounds of the remains of a round tower. Only the featureless stump remains, the upper storeys apparently destroyed by Cromwellian canon in the mid-seventeenth century.

The ruin that stands at Killinaboy today bears little or no resemblance to the original church. The earliest church building may even have been a timber structure. There is no direct evidence for this, but antae (projections of side walls beyond the line of the gable) were traditional features of timber buildings. Stone antae such as those at Killinaboy serve no functional purpose and are generally interpreted as a legacy of traditional timber construction methods. The original stone structure may have included a lintelled doorway in the west gable – nearest the road. This was common in early churches and it is thought that the lintel here may have originally supported the large, double-armed cross that is still one of the most interesting features of the church at Killinaboy. The west gable has been extensively reconstructed. The doorway, if it existed, was not included in the reconstruction, and the cross has been reinserted off-centre. It is impossible to be certain when or why this reconstruction took place, but the original west end, including the cross and the antae, was probably constructed sometime after c. AD 1100, possibly as late as the thirteenth century.[3]

The cross at Killinaboy church is unusual, possibly unique, in Ireland in that it is of a type associated in Medieval Europe with relics and pilgrimage. In this context it fits well with a pattern in contemporary Burren society. Possession of a prestigious relic, such as a fragment of the 'true cross', the bones of a saint or an important crozier or bell, attracted pilgrims and revenue to churches. There seems to have been a network of pilgrimage routes focused on the Burren and pilgrims using such a network would have seen Killinaboy as an important focus for worship.[4]

Another interesting feature of the church at Killinaboy is the carving above the south doorway. Known as a *sheela-na-gig,* it may also support the proposition that Killinaboy was a focus of Medieval pilgrimage. A *sheela-na-gig* is a stone carving of a woman exposing her vagina. They are often found near the access points of castles and churches. Similar figures are known worldwide and are often interpreted as providing protection to a building, its contents or to the people inside by warding off evil. Occasionally found at churches that contained relics, it may be that these carvings were believed to protect the relics.

As well as the double-armed cross in the west gable, Killinaboy is intimately associated with another unusual object known as a Tau cross. This cross was one of three that marked the boundaries of the monastic termon at Killinaboy, but the whereabouts of the other two are not known today. A replica can be found where the original western boundary marker stood at a bend in the road between Killinaboy and Leamaneh Castle; the original is in the Heritage Centre in Corrofin. A Tau cross is not, in fact, a cross, but resembles rather the top of a crutch or staff. It is represented elsewhere in the Burren, notably in a carving on one face of the Doorty Cross at Kilfenora. The Tau cross is used today as a Franciscan symbol.

The Tau cross of Killinaboy has been the subject of much commentary and speculation. One folk myth – that it was carved to record the reconciliation of the O'Brien and O'Quin families after a feud – was dismissed by O'Donovan, who 'scoff[ed] at all this in unmeasured terms of severity'.[5] A carving on a graveslab in the southwest corner of the graveyard at Killinaboy is now believed to be a representation of a crozier with a Tau head, but was thought, at one time, to be 'a curious symbolical (sic) emblem for the parish clerk'.[6] The Tau cross at Killinaboy even disappeared for a short time in the late nineteenth century. According to Rev Dwyer, writing in 1878, 'the person who removed it is not unknown, and if he sets up to be an antiquarian and a gentleman, he had better have it lifted back as quietly as he lifted it away'.[7] The cross was restored to its rightful position in 1894.

The monastic establishment at Killinaboy was subsumed into the diocesan system following the church reforms of the twelfth century. The parish of Killinaboy is first mentioned in taxation lists of 1302–07. Modifications to the church's structure continued until the fifteenth century and much of what can be seen today dates to this period. Apart from the repositioning of the double-armed cross in the west gable, there is further evidence that stones were reused. It is also likely that stones from other buildings were incorporated into the fabric of Killinaboy church. A carved stone just inside the south door is an obvious example, and a sill under a memorial wall plaque in the north wall is very similar to two reused sills in Kilfenora Cathedral.

Located as it is on a route into the Burren, it was inevitable that Killinaboy would witness its share of turmoil during the Medieval period. We have seen that the round tower was almost completely destroyed by Cromwell's forces in the mid-seventeenth century. A century earlier, the church was plundered by one of two warring factions of the O'Brien

Killinaboy Church (note the off-centre east window)

clan. Prior to that, in an earlier O'Brien faction fight in 1317, Dermot O'Brien passed by with his army on his way from Ruan to Corcomroe to do battle with his arch rival Donough O'Brien. Raiding parties regularly passed and probably camped unrecorded on forays into and out of the Burren. Some larger parties were recorded, however, including those of Red Hugh O'Donnell in 1599 and 1600.

All the while, the church was being modified to accommodate changing circumstances. A new round-headed doorway was inserted in the south wall. A slit window between the door and the southwest corner may have been part of the fabric of the original stone church. The fine east window, which is even more noticeably off-centre than the double-armed cross, dates to the fifteenth century. Two gothic windows in the south wall are also late additions.

The north side of the church building is difficult to interpret and has probably been reconstructed and modified a number of times. Given that the cross and east window appear now to be off-centre and that the anta at the west end of the north wall is quite different to that at the end of the south wall, it appears that the whole building may have been enlarged by reconstruction of the north wall north of its original line. There are other examples in the Burren of reconstructed buildings with off-centre gable features.

A lintelled window towards the east end of the north wall at Killinaboy is unlike any other in this church and is a later addition. Indeed, the entire northeast corner appears to have been a late, opportunistic reconstruction with no obvious plan and not much thought evident in its layout. It is the only section of the church to have been constructed with battered walls. The very low doorway at the east end was thought to lead from the outside to an internal burial vault of the O'Quin family.[8] Westropp's alternative suggestion that it was a north porch or vestry door is based on his assertion that the O'Quin family was 'completely broken up' before the fourteenth century and that nobody could claim direct descent at the time when the supposed vault was constructed. Nevertheless, the same Westropp was able to write that the Dysert crozier 'was purchased from an old woman, daughter of an O'Quin, its last hereditary keeper.'[9] The Dysert crozier was acquired by George Petrie, the renowned antiquarian, around 1845. So it appears that there may well have been an O'Quin family vault inside this low doorway at one time.

Two remaining features of interest are to be found in the northeast corner of the church. An arched recess in the east wall at one time framed a panelled slab, but this has since disappeared and the recess has been blocked up.[10] A curious shelf is built into the angle of the north and east walls at about head height. Similar shelves can be found in other Medieval buildings, but their purpose is unclear. The suggestion that this is a corbel seems unlikely; matching corbels would be expected but are absent. A ceiling at this height would also be impractical unless the floor level was considerably lower, and there is no evidence of a room directly above. The attic space may have been occupied, however, as corbel courses on the north and south walls indicate the roof space was floored. An interesting mason's mark can be seen on one of the corbels above and to the left of the apex of the monument built into the north wall. It probably identifies the stonemason who carved the corbels.

The church seems to have fallen into disuse at the beginning of the seventeenth century, the Royal Visitation record of 1615 stating in relation to Killinaboy 'ch and chauncell down'.[11] By the middle of the seventeenth century, the inner walls of the church appear to have been appropriated for commemoration and a number of slabs, plaques, niches and other structures bear witness to the passing of various individuals. By 1712, however, levies were being imposed in Killinaboy and other parishes to fund repairs to Killinaboy church costing £74. Consistorial Court records from 1715 show that levies were as unpopular then as they are now, the list of defaulters on the 1712 levy running to 'ten pages folio, closely written, and include[ing] the largest as well as the smallest holders responsible in the parishes'.[12] Incidentally, the same court records tell of a sentence of excommunication passed on one Wm. Hogan, 'to be read in parish church of Killeneboy [*sic*]… in the midst of Divine service, and when the church was most largely attended'. The charge was 'adultery and being contumacious (contemptuous) in not appearing to answer charge and submit.'

It is not clear whether the defaulters of 1715 foresaw or were the cause of what came next, but by 1718 a new Protestant church was opened in Corrofin and Killinaboy was abandoned.

Parknabinnia and Creevagh Wedge Tombs

Parknabinnia
GR: R 2648 9358

Creevagh
GR: R 2726 9576

Wedge tombs are the most numerous megalithic structures in Ireland, with over 500 examples recorded. They are distributed mainly in the western part of the country and there are concentrations in County Clare and County Cork. In Clare, where about eighty examples have been found, the densest concentration is on Roughan Hill in the Burren. The wedge tomb by the roadside at Parknabinnia, on Roughan Hill, is a very accessible example.

Wedge tombs, dating to the Late Neolithic and Early Bronze Age (c. 2500–2000 BC), were the latest in the sequence of megalithic tomb-building. They are wedge-shaped, with the higher, wider end facing consistently between west and south, and the opposite end being low and narrow. Parknabinnia is typical in this respect. At first sight, it appears to stand symbolic and isolated in similar fashion to portal tombs such as Poulnabrone, but in fact it is only one element of a complex settlement that occupied the area over a long period of time. Roughan Hill slopes away from this wedge tomb to the southwest and the remains of other tombs, stone-built habitation sites and field walls have been found on the hill. Similar evidence can be seen across the Burren uplands stretching away to the northeast, including another wedge tomb at Creevagh, 2.3 km away. This tomb differs from Parknabinnia in that it may have included an outer row of stones and may have been modified some time after first construction. Also, it was later enclosed by a stone-wall that was part of another extensive field system in this area. The walls of this system survive only as low mounds that can still be seen in the area around the tomb and enclosure. The remains of a circular structure, possibly an animal pen, can be seen within the enclosure 15 m west of the tomb.

Incredibly, no Burren wedge tomb has yet been excavated and so conclusions about these two can only be proposed by analogy with others

Entrance to Creevagh wedge tomb

that have been excavated. If they are typical, they were probably used over an extended period and the human remains they contained may have been inhumations or cremations. They may have contained some grave goods such as pottery and stone tools, and if they continued in use into the Bronze Age there may have been moulds or crucibles used for the casting of bronze tools or weapons. They were covered by a mound of stones, the remains of which can be seen, and there may have been a layer of grassy sod covering the mound. Two stones close the entrance to the tomb at Parknabinnia, one of which may have been removable for access. There is a sill stone across the entrance to Creevagh.

What is certain is that the builders of these and other wedge tombs attached some significance to the setting sun. All wedge tombs in Ireland are oriented towards the southwest, and it is possible that variations in orientation may be a factor of the location of the sun when each individual tomb was first planned or laid out.

Rear of Parknabinnia wedge tomb

Cahercommaun
GR: R 2821 9650

The cliff-top stone fort or cashel of Cahercommaun is one of the most impressive monuments in the Burren. A twenty-minute walk is required to reach it, initially on a prepared path and then across bare limestone steps and slab. The effort is well rewarded with spectacular views across the Burren uplands. The cashel itself has a number of unusual features as well as the added benefit of having been professionally excavated and recorded. Dr Hugh O'Neill Hencken conducted the excavation at Cahercommaun over a six-week period in 1934 as part of the Third Harvard Archaeological Expedition in Ireland. The excavation report is useful insofar as it provides a comprehensive record of the huge volume of material recovered by the excavation team.[13] However, much potentially useful information was lost due to the less rigorous excavation and recording standards of the time. Although a number of distinct layers of occupation material were identified, the exact sequence of deposition across the cashel is difficult to reconstruct, and some of Hencken's original conclusions, especially regarding the period of occupation of the cashel, have had to be reinterpreted in light of subsequent discoveries. Nevertheless, the record stands and has been a very valuable starting point in the years since publication.

Any interpretation of the cashel must take account of the contemporary socio-political context. For a detailed description of this context see the section on the Early Medieval period in Chapter 1. In brief, a network of tribute and patronage linked localised tribes or clans with larger and more important groupings loosely referred to as 'kingdoms'. It is likely that Cahercommaun was the focus of an important but minor branch of the kingdom of Cashel that controlled or had a dominant influence over large parts of the Burren in the ninth century AD. The site had been occupied prior to the ninth century. Indeed the entire plateau around Cahercommaun shows evidence of occupation from prehistoric times, and a number of reused prehistoric artefacts are included in the assemblage recorded by Hencken's team. It is impossible to say whether or not the particular site on which the cashel now stands was occupied during the prehistoric period. A number of fifth- and sixth-century artefacts do demonstrate, however, that from this period at least Cahercommaun was seen as suitable for occupation by a small community, estimated by Hencken to have consisted of forty to fifty individuals at its busiest period. There is no evidence that the cashel was occupied after the tenth century.

Cahercommaun is unusual in a number of ways, not just because of its cliff-top location. A cleft running the entire height of the cliff leads from one of the two souterrains within the cashel; the inner wall is massive, containing an estimated 16,500 m^3 of stone;[14] outside this inner wall are two less substantial, roughly concentric walls; the remains of both circular and rectangular stone structures are found within the cashel; it is also possible that there were timber structures that may have been destroyed by fire at some stage late in the period of occupation.

Whereas Hencken divided the occupation into an early and a late phase, a recent re-evaluation of the evidence has proposed three phases of occupation.[15]

Phase A covers the period from the fifth–sixth centuries to the eighth century. The earliest settlers may have occupied a small, flimsy enclosure containing one or more structures, possibly some of those next to the northern section of the present inner wall (nearest the cliff). If there was an enclosure, it may subsequently have been demolished or incorporated into the present inner cashel wall. The only evidence of occupation during this period consists of a number of metal objects such as brooches and pins that are known by association with similar objects found elsewhere in Ireland to have been in use during this timeframe. Also, the way occupation material was deposited within some of the internal structures and in the area of the two souterrains suggests a settlement phase prior to construction of the souterrains.

Phase B represents the high point of activity and status in the ninth century, and the present walls, together with the complex of circular structures in the northern half of the cashel all date to this period. The souterrains were built (one with its entrance inside the principal structure of this phase) and concealed under a platform that was backfilled over the remains of the earlier structures at the north wall. The entrance to the cashel, which runs under the modern boardwalk and viewing platform, consisted of a narrow paved passageway extending through both outer walls. It was itself walled on both sides, but it is impossible to know how high the side walls were. What is certain, based on evidence from similar cashels elsewhere, is that the entrance passageway through the inner cashel wall formed an 8 m tunnel, roofed with large capstones to support the weight of material above. A second complex of structures, built just inside the entrance, has been interpreted as a guard chamber accessed by means of a narrow passageway. The cashel wall was terraced on the inside. The remains of two of these terraces can still be seen, but it seems probable that there were more and that the inner wall was considerably higher than it appears today. The terraces were accessed by means of ladders supported in specially constructed niches in the wall, and again, some of these niches can still be seen opposite the viewing platform.

The outer walls are intriguing. Cahercommaun has been referred to as a tri-vallate (three-walled) fort and it has been suggested on this basis that it was a 'royal' or at least a very high-status site. This seems unlikely, however. While the inner wall is massive and clearly constructed with defence in mind, the middle and outer walls are so comparatively flimsy and poorly constructed that they could scarcely provide any obstacle to determined attack. At least nine vertical joins in the outer wall, some of which can still be seen, were weak points that would be easy to exploit to breach the wall. The fact that, in addition to these walls, the area outside the cashel is divided by a number of radial walls gives the impression more of domestic than defensive purpose.

A 'royal' site would be expected to have yielded a much richer inventory of artefacts than was recovered from Cahercommaun. No gold was found here other than traces used for decoration of individual artefacts. The most exotic piece was a much used silver brooch recovered from the floor of one of the souterrains. Other objects that could loosely be classed as jewellery were of iron, copper alloy, bone and glass/lignite – hardly status materials.

An enormous quantity of animal bone was recovered from within the cashel. Sheep, goat, pig, horse, red deer and other species were represented, but by far the largest proportion of bone (97 per cent, or 4,183 kg) was of cattle. The bone was scattered evenly throughout the cashel and accumulated with other occupation material to such an extent that, by the time the settlement was abandoned, ground level within the cashel had been raised by about 1.5 m above the original bedrock. Large numbers of domestic tools and fittings, such as iron knives and shears and various types of spindle whorl give the clear impression that this was a busy, functional site. Many of the iron knives had been continuously resharpened, and the presence of dozens of pieces of iron slag at all levels indicates that Cahercommaun was a self-sufficient production centre throughout Phase B of its occupation.

It is unclear how long Phase B lasted, but it may have been less than a century. Phase C saw the reflooring of the southern part of the cashel

Cahercommaun – vertical join in outer wall

and extension and re-alignment of the inner section of the entrance passageway to lead directly towards a new rectangular structure that was built at the centre of the cashel. The circular structures of Phase B appear to have been abandoned in favour of the new rectangular structure, and it is possible that a general deterioration during this phase necessitated the construction of the low outer buttress supporting a bulging section of the main cashel wall on the southwest. Occupation material continued to accumulate on the new floor in the southern section, eventually covering the lowest terrace and leading to the use of the ladder niches as hearths. The cashel was finally abandoned sometime in the tenth century.

It would appear, therefore, given the layout described above and the socio-political context of the period, that the cashel as we see it today was an important staging post in the network of tribute and patronage that linked the Burren with the kingdom of Cashel in the ninth century. Cahercommaun seems to have been occupied by a privileged dynasty (the *Uí Chormaic* [ee kurmic]) that arrived from an area south of the River Shannon during the preceding century. Though they were defeated militarily in the eighth century by the 'native' clan (the *Corcu Modruadh* [kurku mruah]), they appear to have retained responsibility for collecting tribute from the natives. The tribute levied on the *Corcu Modruadh,* which according to surviving records included 300 beef cattle, 300 milch cows, 300 boars and 300 cloaks (possibly sheep), gives an indication of how busy the settlement at Cahercommaun must have been during its heyday. It also suggests that, far from being defensive in the military sense, the middle and outer walls enclosed holding pens for the many animals that would have been gathered together at Cahercommaun as part of the tribute network.

The abandonment of Cahercommaun probably coincided with the decline of the *Uí Chormaic* and the advance of a new grouping, the *Dál gCais* [dhawl gash], that would dominate the Burren in the following centuries.

Fulacht Fiadh, Fahee South
GR: R 2919 9885

The monument by the roadside in the townland of Fahee South, about 1 km east of Carran, has been referred to since its discovery and excavation in the late 1980s as a *fulacht fiadh* [fullokht feeah] and it is one of about 300 such monuments known in County Clare. This was one of the earliest excavations of a *fulacht fiadh,* and it was unusual in that it was for a long time one of the few *fulachta fiadh* in the country to have yielded animal remains – in this case cow, deer and horse. Current investigations elsewhere in the country are, however, revealing more frequent associations with animal bones. The Burren *fulachta fiadh* are also slightly unusual in that the mounds consist of limestone. This is not surprising given the local geology, but the material used in a large proportion of these monuments elsewhere in Ireland was sandstone.

Archaeologists tend now to use the generic name 'burnt mounds' to describe these monuments. *Fulachta fiadh* are probably a subset of the type, specifically cooking places where large joints of meat were boiled in troughs or roasted in pits or chambers. Given the possible evidence of butchering of the bones discovered at this particular site, it is likely that it was indeed used for cooking. For a general description of *fulachta fiadh,* see the section on the Bronze Age in Chapter 1.

It is difficult to see the outline from the road. It appears as no more than a grass-covered mound with the open section giving access to the central trough facing away from the road. As expected, it is often waterlogged; it is at one of the lowest points of the Carran turlough, and indeed the nearby road is regularly impassable in wet weather. Though drainage patterns may have been different during the Bronze Age, it would not have been unusual for such a monument to be constructed in a place where it could only be used sporadically. Occasionally, trackways and platforms were constructed by the users of waterlogged burnt mounds to provide access and stable footing, but no evidence of such an arrangement was found here.[16]

Templecronan
GR: M 2889 0000

Templecronan has to be one of the most charming monuments in the Burren. Located out of sight in a hollow, a short walk from the nearest road, it is one of those monuments that is not often visited and is therefore not as well known as its more accessible neighbours. Its present-day remoteness belies its earlier status, however; in its day it was a monastic settlement and an important focus of pilgrimage.

Tradition has it that the monastery was founded in the seventh century by St Cronan, possibly the same Cronan who founded the larger monastery at Roscrea, County Tipperary. If this is the case, the earliest structure is likely to have been of timber, but since no archaeological excavation has been conducted here, it is impossible to say this for certain. Some features of the present stone church lead, as we shall see, to other questions about its construction. The settlement consisted, in its heyday, of the church, two shrines, a termon, at least one termon cross, a holy well and a number of domestic structures. Traces of the termon boundary may possibly remain in the curved walls to the north and south of the church. The outlines of some of the domestic buildings are traced in the low mound walls in the field outside the north termon boundary; a deep, regular depression in the same field to the northeast of the domestic buildings is probably a quarry from which the large stones of the church were extracted.

A holy well located at the base of a small cliff about 100 m south of the church may have marked a contemporary southern approach to the settlement. Another approach from the northwest was marked by a termon cross.

The church itself is a small single-room oratory. It is built in the very early, pre-twelfth-century style, but includes features that are characteristically post-twelfth century. The walls, particularly those at south and east, are constructed with massive stone blocks in a style known today as cyclopean. A fine example of this style can be found at Oughtmama where the western church includes early, closely fitted cyclopean masonry. The trabeate doorway in the west wall of Templecronan is another characteristically early form, with jambs sloping inwards towards the top under a large stone lintel. Another early feature is the tiny window in the east wall. Viewed from the outside, it appears as no more than a slit in the wall. However, a decorated embrasure makes the window appear much larger from the inside, and the lower part forms a shelf on which the host or chalice, or possibly a relic of some sort, may have been placed for veneration. The decorated stone forming the lower part of the right jamb of the embrasure was almost certainly matched on the left; though all trace of the unusual button decoration has fractured off the front face, the stone on the left was moulded in a similar fashion to the right and includes similar vertical incised lines on the inner face of the embrasure. Similar, though more delicately carved stones have been reused in a churchyard wall at Rath Blathmac [raw blomock], about 3 km southwest of Corrofin. They may originally have been used within the church and could indicate a pattern in church decoration. However, it is more likely that the Rath Blathmac stones were used originally in the nearby tower house or in a round tower that is supposed to have stood within the churchyard. The Templecronan example is less refined and probably earlier, and in the absence of further evidence any connection must remain entirely speculative.[17]

Despite the evidence for an early date for construction of Templecronan, a number of features indicate that it may have been partially rebuilt after the twelfth century. The carved human and animalistic heads dotted around the church walls, and the carved corbels at each corner, are more than likely later additions, although the carved stone forming part of the left jamb of the west doorway is difficult to explain if the doorway is earlier. A corresponding carving on the opposite side of the doorway looks like a later insertion. A total of six or seven carved human and stylised heads can be seen, one high on the outside of the south wall, three on the outside of the west wall (two at the door jambs) and one above the door in the north wall. A further probable example is represented today by a projecting stone inside the church near the east end of the north wall, but no trace of carving remains on this. The small V-shaped stone just inside the north door may be contemporary with the fifteenth-century insertion of the doorway. It is remarkably similar to a possible font in a wall of the chancel of the western church at Oughtmama, but it may have been another in the series of head carvings that adorn the walls of Templecronan.

A number of other carved stones are notable. The roll-moulded quoins at the southeast, southwest and northwest corners are uncommon in church buildings in the Burren and show remarkable attention to detail in an early church.

The present entrance to the church is a fifteenth-century Gothic doorway inserted in the north wall. The inner opening of the doorway is rectangular to accommodate an inward opening timber door that was hinged between the surviving spud-stone and hanging eye.

Templecronan

Tobar Fachtnan
GR: M 3004 0047

As described elsewhere in this guide, the tradition of visiting spring wells pre-dates Christianity, but the practice was incorporated into the Irish church and holy wells have been visited since early Christian times by pilgrims.

St Fachtnan's Well near Carran village is one of the many holy wells to be found in the Burren and should not be confused with a holy well of the same name at Kilfenora. In fact, the designation of the present well may be erroneous. The 1916 edition of the Ordnance Survey 6-inch map calls it *Tobernafiaghanta* [thubber na feeantha], a designation that corresponds with that given by the contemporary local antiquarian Dr G. U. MacNamara. This is translated as 'The Well of the Hunters'.[18] The name in the Irish language is given as *Tobar na Féachanta* [thubber na faykantha]. This term refers to sight or vision and corresponds with a 1977 note attributed to the author Tim Robinson on *The Placenames Database of Ireland* – 'This is an eye-well with penitential stations said to be dedicated to St Fachtna.'

Whatever about the name, the well itself fits neatly in the pilgrimage tradition, the more so because it is associated with an adjacent group of penitential stations. These are carefully constructed dry-stone markers, up to 2 m high, that were used to mark the 'rounds' walked by pilgrims at the site. It is likely that these stations were on one or more of the pilgrimage routes in the Burren. A holy well at Glencolumbkille, 2 km to the southeast, is at the foot of one of the few natural passes from the east into the Burren. At the top of this pass is another group of penitential stations. About 1.5 km southwest of Tobar Fachtnan is Templecronan church, a pilgrimage destination since Medieval times. A second natural route (from the northeast) would also have led the Templecronan-bound pilgrim by Tobar Fachtnan.

Mac Duagh's Hermitage

Church
GR: M 3289 0424

Servant's Grave
GR: M 3331 0409

Bóthar na Mias
GR: M 3329 0432

Asceticism was a feature of the early Irish church, and one of the earliest recorded ascetics was St Colman Mac Duagh. Born sometime around the middle of the sixth century, not much is known of his early life, other than that he studied for about fifteen years under the guidance of St Enda on Inis Mór, one of the Aran Islands off the Burren coast. Life on the island was not, apparently, isolated enough for him and in AD 592 he returned to the mainland to find a suitable place to live the life of a hermit. With a servant or companion, he found a cave at the base of a cliff under Slieve Carran where he lived in seclusion for the next seven years. Nothing is known of this period of his life other than through legends that have long been associated with him.

One of these legends concerns his daily routine of prayer and study. By this account, he was helped in maintaining a punishing regime by three companions – a cock, a mouse and a fly. The cock used to rouse him from his sleep early in the morning, whereupon he would embark on a long day of prayer and study of his sacred scripture. So as not to lose his place in the text while he broke during the day for more prayer or to eat, he would point to the line he had reached on the page, where the fly would alight and remain until he was ready to resume his study. Such a demanding routine would have left the hermit exhausted by the end of the day, but discipline forbade him to sleep through the night. The cock, naturally, was off-duty during the hours of darkness and so St Colman recruited a mouse to nibble his ear during the night to wake him for prayer.

Another legend associated with the saint concerns his decision eventually to abandon the eremitic life and return to the mainstream church.

St Colman was a cousin of Guaire [gooreh], King of Aidhne [eye-neh], the region of southeast Galway bordering the Burren. Guaire's stronghold was located not far from the tower house known today as *Dún Guaire* [doon gooreh], just outside the modern village of Kinvara, about 8 km from St Colman's hermitage. At Easter in the seventh year of his retreat, as St Colman and his servant were preparing their frugal meal, his royal cousin was preparing to celebrate Easter in more sumptuous style. Saying the blessing before the meal, the king asked the Lord, should there be anybody more deserving, to let him have the food that had been prepared. The Lord obliged, and everything on the table floated out the window heading south. The king summoned his horse and guards and set off in pursuit. As they approached the cliff at Slieve Carran, the dishes, goblets, cruets and cutlery landed on a flat section of rock where St Colman and his servant were about to start their own meal. The king, with his pursuing horses and guards, were rooted to the spot and could not move until the two hermits had thanked the Lord for his benevolence and eaten their fill. The impressions of the crockery from the table, together with those of hooves and feet of horses and soldiers, can be seen to this day at *Bóthar na Mia*s [bow-her na meeas] – the 'Road of the Vessels' – not far from the hermitage. King Guaire, recognising his long-lost cousin, and acknowledging the judgement of the Lord, offered to endow a monastery if St Colman agreed to be abbot. The site for the new monastery would be indicated by a sign. And so it happened that as he was walking some time later not far from his old hermitage, St Colman's belt fell to the ground at the site now known as Kilmacduagh, near Gort, County Galway, one of the most important ecclesiastical sites in the area.

Both these legends are commemorated in stained glass windows by George Walsh Sr at Tirneevin Church, 2 km north of Kilmacduagh.

Unfortunately, despite the founding of an impressive monastery, the legend has an unhappy ending. St Colman's servant was made of less stern stuff than his master and, following seven years of deprivation, his body was unable to handle the rich food of the meal and he died. The grieving saint laid him to rest a short distance away; the grave can still be seen 400 m south of the hermitage.

The hermitage consists today of a small stone oratory, two *leachtanna* [lockthanna], a holy well, the cave and a bullaun [bullawn] stone. It is hidden away among the trees and hazel scrub at the base of *Cinn Áille* [keen awlieh], a sheer cliff face forming the eastern flank of Slieve Carran. *Bóthar na Mias* and the Servant's Grave can be found in open ground to the east of the hermitage. The oratory is a small stone structure, very dilapidated and impossible to date accurately. If St Colman built an oratory here, it certainly was not this one, as the earliest stone churches did not appear in Ireland until over a century later. The fact that it is here at all, however, reinforces the accounts of St Colman's retreat; it is difficult to imagine a purpose for an early church in such a remote location other than as a focus for pilgrimage. The cave and holy well have attracted pilgrims from early times, and the tradition is maintained to this day with an annual pilgrimage on 21 October. *Leachtanna* and bullaun stones have traditionally been associated with pilgrimage, the former used as altars or penitential stations and the latter as holy water fonts. The assorted stones that lay on top of one of the *leachtanna* (described by T. J. Westropp sometime between 1910 and 1913) may have been used by pilgrims to count their rounds, but unfortunately they have long since disappeared.

Slightly north of the route to the hermitage is a Bronze Age *fulacht fiadh* at Keelhilla (GR: R 3302 0370). As is the case with most monuments of this type, it can be difficult to recognise on the ground and to get to without the help of GPS. If this one proves to be elusive, there is another example near Carran village that is described elsewhere in this guide (Fulacht Fiadh, Fahee South).

Mac Duagh's hermitage – entrance to cave

3. Burren North

Turlough Hill

Hillfort
GR: M 3142 0732

Settlement
GR: M 3059 0695

Cairn
GR: M 3033 0682

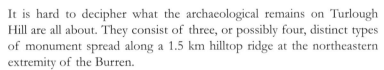

It is hard to decipher what the archaeological remains on Turlough Hill are all about. They consist of three, or possibly four, distinct types of monument spread along a 1.5 km hilltop ridge at the northeastern extremity of the Burren.

At the northeastern end of the ridge is a large (225 m in diameter) stone-built enclosure that resembles superficially a type of Bronze Age monument known as a hillfort. However, whereas most Bronze Age hillforts appear to have been defended habitations, the builders of this structure paid scant regard to defence. Hillforts are generally surrounded by two or three outer ramparts – there are none surrounding this one – with the entrances to the fort constructed in such a way as to be easily defended from the inside. The present breaches in the stone wall on Turlough Hill may or may not all be original, but one obvious entrance (at the east) relies only on a natural fault in the bedrock to provide a defensible passageway to the interior.

An alternative explanation for this monument is that it is a symbolic meeting place dating to the earlier Neolithic period. It commands a strategic position at the edge of the Burren overlooking one of the few natural approaches from the east, and affords spectacular views over the surrounding landscape. Given the importance of landscape in prehistoric times, it is plausible that this was a central, occasional gathering place for different tribes or other groupings, perhaps for celebration or trade at important times of the year.

About 600 m away to the southwest, on a distinct natural bedrock terrace, there are the faint remains of a large group of at least 165 stone huts. This collection is truly enigmatic and almost without parallel anywhere else in the country. A similar complex at Mullaghfarna, County Sligo (consisting of 153 huts on a limestone plateau) has produced both Neolithic and Early Bronze Age dates, but archaeological material recovered there had been washed down into grykes and so was of limited use for dating. Were these huts temporary or permanent? How were they roofed? Why so many in such a small location?

A large cairn of stones can be found towards the southwestern end of the bedrock terrace on which the huts were constructed. Cairns are not uncommon; there are other examples in the Burren (including Poulawack and Slieve Carran) and throughout the country. Some cover prehistoric burials while others appear to be symbolic (though many of the currently unexcavated cairns may in time prove to be burial mounds). Some also include outer kerbs while others do not. The cairn at Turlough Hill has not yet been excavated, so it is impossible to be sure of its significance. What is clear, however, is that it differs structurally from the cairn at Poulawack in that it does not include an outer kerb of slabs. Also, though now partially collapsed along much of its circumference, the remaining intact facing indicates that it was probably significantly higher than Poulawack. Furthermore, it makes a much more emphatic statement in the landscape than Poulawack, and appears closer in this regard to a cairn on Slieve Carran than Poulawack.

T. J. Westropp, puzzled by Turlough Hill at the turn of the nineteenth century, wrote: 'It only remains for me to describe and illustrate it, and to leave the solution (if any) to later antiquaries.'[1]

A current research project, conducted by the Department of Archaeology at the National University of Ireland, Galway, is seeking to answer some of the riddles of Turlough Hill. Already, surveys have revealed a previously unrecognised, low-profile enclosure with surrounding walls or banks on the eastern part of the summit.

Burren North

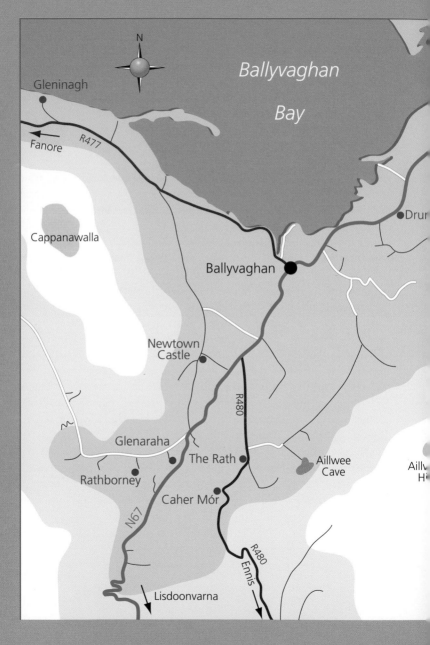

Turlough Hill cairn and possible habitation site

Oughtmama

Monastic Settlement GR: M 3053 0785	

Tobar Cholmáin GR: M 3114 0818	

Oughtmama is an early monastic settlement showing signs of modification, possibly over a period of four to five centuries. It consists principally of three churches surrounded by a double enclosure, some domestic buildings and gardens, a mill race and the site of a water-mill, a *leacht* (a rectangular stone structure thought to have been used as an outdoor altar) and a holy well. The present pattern of fields surrounding the enclosures dates, in part, to the time of occupation of the settlement.

The name of the settlement derives from two Irish words – *ucht* [ukth] meaning breast and *maum* [mawm] meaning a high pass – and so refers to its location just below one of the few mountain passes leading into the Burren from the east. The pass referred to is most likely the one directly east of the settlement, between Turlough Hill and Oughtmama Hill; the presence of a holy well between the settlement and the pass indicates that this may have been a pilgrimage route, and similar associations between ecclesiastical sites, holy wells and access routes can be seen elsewhere in the eastern Burren. It is unusual to find the word *maum* used in the Burren – it is more usually associated with place names in Connemara like Maam, Maumturk and Maumtrasna. The fact that it is used to refer to one of the northernmost routes into the Burren may indicate the use of this particular route by pilgrims from the Galway/Connemara region.

The Churches

Two of the churches are within the inner enclosure and the third is a short distance away between the inner and outer enclosures. The western church is the oldest; it is impossible to date its foundation accurately, but it was probably constructed sometime around AD 1100 as a one-room oratory. It was enlarged in the early thirteenth century by the addition of a chancel to the east. This was also the period during which the other two churches were added, one inside and one outside the inner enclosure. Since there has been no archaeological excavation at Oughtmama, we can only speculate about the exact sequence of construction, but it would seem plausible that after an initial foundation and consolidation phase, the early thirteenth century saw an improvement in the fortunes of the settlement, an expansion of the monastic community and the development of a supporting infrastructure.

The Western Church

The western church is the largest of the three. The north wall is remarkably well constructed, with huge, well trimmed blocks of stone laid in irregular courses. This style is common in early churches, but the standard of workmanship in this case is particularly fine. The style is known as cyclopean, a term used to describe 'every architectural work of extraordinary magnitude, to the execution of which human labour appeared inadequate'; in other words the blocks of stone were so large that they must have been put in place by giants like the Cyclops![2]

There is some evidence available to suggest a sequence of modification for this church:

Oughtmama Churches

- The masonry style of the eastern section of the north wall is different from that of the rest of the building; the blocks of stone are larger and were trimmed more carefully so that there is very little space between the blocks. In contrast, spall was used extensively to fill the joints in the western section. The original church would appear, therefore, to have been extended westwards some time after its original construction.

- The original section of the north wall was built on a plinth that can still be seen. Assuming that the plinth extended under the whole of the original building, we would expect to find it under the south wall. We would also expect the eastern section of the south wall to be of similar fine construction to the opposite north wall. It is not. There may indeed be a plinth concealed below the present surface at the south wall, but if there is not, this would be a good indication that the church was widened at some point.

- The church may not have been extended until some time after it had been widened. The top of the arch of the Romanesque east window in the south wall has been removed to accommodate a lower side wall, yet the west window in the same wall is fully accommodated in the lower wall.

- The small original stone church probably included a crude east window, possibly similar in style to that at Templecronan. This appears to have been replaced by a large, finely carved Romanesque window, which was in turn discarded when the chancel was built. The head and base of this large window can now be seen on the ground beside the church. Incidentally, the head of the window, lying to the west of the church, is reputed to provide 'a sovereign cure for headaches if the patient lies down and inserts his head into it.'[3]

- Since the chancel arch and west doorway are more or less centred in their respective walls, they would have been constructed either at the same time as, or after, the church was widened. A difficulty with this interpretation, however, is that lintelled doorways generally pre-date the twelfth-century introduction of the Romanesque style. Perhaps the original was simply reconstructed in the new gable wall.

- It is possible that the small window in the south wall of the middle church is the original window of the western church; its crude style is out of character with the rest of the middle church. If this is correct, the construction of the middle church may be contemporary with the modification of the western church, when the large Romanesque window was inserted into the east wall.

Inside the door of the western church are two holy water fonts, one of which has an unusual carving, described as follows:

> In the southwest interior angle of the church, a small stoup of stone projects from the wall. It was once used as a font for holding holy water, and the front of it is curiously ornamented with carving, representing in relief some fanciful fabulous animals, covered with scales, and entwined together by the necks. One of them appears to have no less than six feet, two of which the people of the neighbourhood denominate tails. From this circumstance, the whole tank has acquired the appellation, Cathastaurable, or the cat with two tails, derived from Cat, a cat, Da, two, and Earbull, a tail.[1]

A less Victorian eye might have acknowledged the obvious, which is that these animals are male, and not endowed with two tails.

The doorway is constructed in the early, lintelled style. Above the doorway is the hanging eye used to hinge the wooden door of the church. A hanging eye such as this would have had a corresponding spud-stone at ground level, but no trace remains today.

The chancel includes two windows, one in the east wall above the altar and a second, probably dating to the fifteenth century, in the south wall. The embrasure (the splayed interior) of this latter window consists of finely carved limestone blocks with typical fifteenth-century diagonal dressing. Also in the south wall of the chancel is a curious carved font set into the wall between the window and the east wall.

The Middle Church

The middle church is a smaller, one-roomed building, constructed on a plinth, with single windows in the east and south walls. That in the south wall is crudely constructed and, as discussed above, may be the original window of the western church. The east window, in contrast, consists of carved, rebated limestone blocks and is similar to the windows in the south wall of the western church. It is much more impressive from the inside than the outside. Unlike the doorway of the larger church, that of the middle church is arched, indicating a twelfth century or later date.

The Eastern Church

The eastern church is also built on a plinth, but is in a much poorer state of repair. Nevertheless, the east window remains substantially intact and the remains of the doorway, in this case in the south wall, can still be seen. This church is not aligned with the other two and is outside the inner, or sacred, part of the site. Why it was set apart is unclear, but it may have been a nun's or Lady Chapel, or possibly simply for the lay members of the community.

The Settlement

The enclosure walls are difficult to identify in places, but part of the western section of the inner wall can be seen in the field to the west of the churches about 20 m beyond the *leacht*. The outer enclosure is 50–100 m outside the inner.

The outlines of the domestic buildings (referred to on the 1842 Ordnance Survey map as Oughtmama Town) are about 100 m to the east of the churches; together with the mill race, terraced garden and a possible rubbish dump or midden, they suggest that a substantial, self-sufficient community occupied the settlement.[5] Horizontal wheel-mills were in use in Ireland from at least the middle of the seventh century and it would not have been unusual to find a mill at a community such as Oughtmama.[6] The mill race was fed by the surface run-off from the surrounding hills and from a spring well, the present St Colman's holy well, about 700 m away to the north-east.

The surrounding land was farmed by the community. The pattern of long narrow fields surrounding the settlement is now only hinted at in the traces of field walls to the north of the western church. It is reflected, albeit more dramatically, around the contemporary Cistercian abbey of Corcomroe directly across the valley. By laying their fields out in this manner, the monks were simply being efficient – the teams of animals used for ploughing did not need to be turned as often! Describing the echo in the valley, Cooke has this to say:

When the tourist stations himself outside, and to the south of the church fronting Knockocallaghan mountain, a single shout is, in favourable weather, so loudly and oft repeated, that it resembles the loud burst of a pack of fox-hounds in full cry; a bugle blast is magnified into a complete band; and the discharge of a fowling-piece, into the continued roar of many pieces of ordnance.

No person visiting this part of the country should leave it without provoking Echo from her slumbers here.[7]

Tobar Cholmáin

Tobar Cholmáin, St Colman's Well, lies 700 m to the northeast of the settlement, about halfway up the hill towards the pass between Oughtmama Hill and Turloughmore Hill. It is marked by a lone wind-blown tree, which an imaginative mind might say has arched over the well to protect it.

The Ordnance Survey Letters of 1839 include the following extract about St Colman's Well: 'This well is indued with extraordinary naturally medicinal, or supernaturally miraculous virtues, for people have often washed their eyes in it, which were veiled with thick pearls, and ere they had completed the third washing these pearls (films) fell off leaving the eyes perfectly bright and clear-sighted.'[8]

It is still visited by people looking for a cure for eye ailments, and votive offerings can often be seen laid by the well or tied to the tree. 'Pattern Day', the traditional annual day of pilgrimage, is on 15 November.

Tobar Cholmáin – holy well dedicated to St Colman

Corcomroe Abbey
GR: M 2950 0898

Corcomroe Abbey is one of the treasures of the Burren. Not only is it impressive in scale and detail, it also narrates a fascinating story of society in general and of the Cistercian community in particular in the twelfth and subsequent centuries. The abbey is exceptional in a number of ways in comparison with contemporary church buildings in the Burren, including location, size, architecture and decoration. It also fits neatly into an historical pattern of spiritual/secular relationships and the peculiar development of the Medieval Irish church. The Irish Cistercian houses of the period were a troublesome lot, and Corcomroe was no exception.

It is impossible to state with certainty when, or by whom, Corcomroe was founded. The best guess is that it was founded some time around 1194 by Dónal Mór O'Brien or his son Donough Cairbreach. These men were chieftains of the powerful O'Brien family that, by the time the monastic orders began to come to Ireland in the first half of the twelfth century, had established itself as one of the dominant families in the region. Construction of the new abbey at Corcomroe may not have begun until about 1205, but by 1210 it appears to have been well under way.

T. L. Cooke, writing in 1842, believed that the western part of the church was built first, presumably on the basis that the construction is crude and haphazard and could only have improved as the builders gained more experience and worked eastwards to the visibly more refined eastern end. However, this ignores the fact that Cistercian masons were already very skilled and experienced builders by the time they arrived in Ireland in 1142. In fact, it was the chancel at the eastern end of the church that was built first in a style now known as 'Transitional'. This includes elements of Romanesque and Gothic styles, such as Romanesque round-headed windows and Gothic pointed windows. It is characterised by finely cut and carefully fitted stone, with finely worked moulding around windows and doors. It is a distinct style used by a group of contemporary stonemasons in the west of Ireland (now known as the 'School of the West'), and elements of the style can be seen in other buildings in the Burren, such as Kilfenora Cathedral and Noughaval church.

Though locally impressive in scale, Corcomroe is by no means large in comparison with other Cistercian abbeys. Vaucelles in Normandy, for example, is more than three times the size and Corcomroe cannot match the refinement of the finest Continental or English abbeys. Nevertheless, the style and standard of construction is reasonably consistent throughout the chancel and the Cistercian fondness for symmetry is generally respected. However, all was not well in Corcomroe in the early thirteenth century, and almost from the beginning this particular abbey seemed to develop a character of its own. In laying out the foundations for the chancel, a mistake was made, the result of which was that the whole chancel arch was skewed on completion. The northern base of the arch is approximately 25 cm west of where it should be – hardly noticeable to the untrained eye, but not what one would expect in a Cistercian abbey. A further mistake was made during construction of the chancel, the effect of which can be seen at the top of the small single window in the east wall. If only for aesthetic reasons, the top of the window should be below the line of the rib vault (ceiling) of the chancel. The fact that it is not indicates that either two teams worked independently on east wall and chancel vault, or that whoever had overall responsibility for construction was not up to the job and got his measurements wrong.

Cistercians were in the habit of carefully laying out their plans before and during construction. The masons even used templates to guide cutting of individual stones. The earliest known templates are at Byland Abbey in Yorkshire, and traces of templates used by the masons at Corcomroe can still be found in the plasterwork of the north wall of the north transept and the north wall of the south transept chapel. The Cistercians were knowledgeable metallurgists and they understood how to make and use the saws that were needed to cut hard limestone precisely to shape. While they waited for the masons to convert their designs into finished pieces, the architects may have relieved boredom by doodling on the walls; a freehand drawing of a sailboat can be seen etched into the plaster below and to the right of the 'smiling bishop' wall plaque in the chancel.

Apart from the two architectural mistakes referred to above, the lack of a coherent plan is reflected in other ways that can be seen as you walk around the building; the different styles of window in the north and south transept chapels; alterations made to the roofline during construction; the south transept chapel arch being lower than the north; decorative details that should be symmetrical across the centre-line of the church but are not. Why the north wall of the nave should have been built with three arches and the south with two (and these not aligned in any way) is a mystery. Why the grandeur of the east window should be

Corcomroe Abbey – chancel and east window
(courtesy Mark Carthy)

reflected in the otherwise poorly constructed west end of the church is another. Perhaps the skilled masons who were employed at the beginning of construction carved the stonework for the west window and left it on site for later insertion after they had departed. Or perhaps a subsequent group of labourers were unable to match the skill of their predecessors. Whatever about the design elements of construction, the method also tells a story. If you stand to the south side of the building in line with the bell tower, the difference in the quality and style of construction between the eastern (chancel) end and the west end is striking. In contrast with the finely worked stone of the chancel, the nave appears almost crude. 'Putlog holes' dot the walls of the nave, attesting to the use of timber scaffolding during construction. Timber beams were laid across the walls to support platforms used by the builders and were left in place as the walls got higher. Putlog holes remain in the fabric of the walls after the scaffolding has been cut away and the sections of the timber beams left in the walls have decayed. If scaffolding was used during construction of the chancel, the builders were obviously concerned to ensure that it would not interfere with the finished result; no putlog holes can be seen in the east end of the building. Within the nave itself, the quality of workmanship is generally poor, deteriorating from the eastern section towards the southwest corner. This nave has been described as 'among the worst pieces of Cistercian building in Europe'.[9]

Why all this happened is not fully understood. It could simply have been that a new abbot was appointed, less experienced or with different priorities than the original, who perhaps moved on to begin construction of a daughter house at Kilshane, County Limerick. It could also have been that, having established the routine of construction, supervision and the traditional Cistercian discipline were relaxed. The most likely explanation for the decline in building quality is, however, that the Cistercian Order simply found it too difficult to maintain its normal standards in such a remote and difficult province as Ireland. Language was a serious barrier to the French-speaking monks who came to Ireland to help found the early abbeys, as it was for those appointed to come on later supervision visits. Irish monks and lay brothers did not fully embrace the silent, frugal and austere Cistercian way. The monks, like their lay compatriots, resented outside interference in the traditional way of life following the Anglo-Norman invasion of 1169. The Gaelic abbeys, those affiliated to Mellifont as distinct from their Anglo-Norman counterparts, were in effect appropriated by their patrons for their own benefit and took on something resembling a traditional Gaelic character in terms of both religious observance and construction.

What is certain is that the early thirteenth century in Ireland was a time of strife, famine and plague. The congregation plummeted. The monastic community and the surrounding land on which it depended was vulnerable – 'churches and lay properties were plundered and its clerics and men of skill driven to far foreign regions'.[10] It is not hard to imagine that in such difficult times, with danger all around, economic activity in decline and the focus on survival, grand projects would have slipped well down the list of priorities. Nevertheless, Corcomroe continued as a functioning Cistercian abbey through the thirteenth and fourteenth centuries. It is mentioned in Papal documents, and its abbots had responsibilities in church administration beyond the confines of Corcomroe itself. But it developed in that peculiarly Irish fashion that had been characteristic since the first arrival of Christianity in Ireland 800 years previously. It was intimately involved in and influenced by the secular establishment. Specific contemporary references are scarce, but there can be no doubt that Corcomroe functioned as much for the benefit of its patrons as for the glory of God and the broader Cistercian community. Despite having been granted a dispensation, abbots did not feel bound to attend General Chapters of the Cistercian Order in France as often as they were required to. Complaints were made to no less an authority than Pope Gregory IX about the abuses and lack of discipline in the Irish Cistercian community. The fact that Corcomroe was built in the Gaelic heartland rather than under the direct influence of the Anglo-Norman administration reinforced its insularity.

The 'Gaelic' Cistercians were always in danger of becoming a sect and, indeed, their defiance escalated after 1217 when a visiting delegation sent by the Cistercian General Chapter was refused entry at Mellifont. Resistance to interference from outside spread countrywide and is now known as the 'Conspiracy of Mellifont'. Subsequent visits at other monasteries often turned violent; entrances were blocked, delegations attacked, monasteries besieged and the general impression is one of chaos. While there is no direct evidence of resistance at Corcomroe during the 'Conspiracy of Mellifont', the abbey did not escape the 'solution' to the crisis imposed by Stephen of Lexington in 1228. He dissolved the network of relationships among the Irish monasteries – the Mellifont affiliation – and placed them directly under the control of 'reliable' monasteries in England, Wales and France. Corcomroe became a daughter house of Furness in Lancashire. Even then, however, the community at Corcomroe sought to preserve its independence and a delegation from the new mother house was refused entry in 1231.

Religious strife was not the only danger that the monks at Corcomroe had to contend with during the thirteenth and fourteenth centuries. Constructed as it was on one of the few natural routeways into and out of the northern part of the Burren, it attracted every 'army' and raiding party that saw an opportunity in the region. If you look northeast you can see the route up to the Corker Pass between Abbey Hill on the left and Oughtmama Hill on the right, and there are numerous accounts from the period recording expeditionary groups passing by, availing of the hospitality of the monks, engaging in battle and leaving their dead behind for burial. An elaborate tomb, generally believed to be that of Conor *na Siúdaine* [shoodhinna] O'Brien, King of Thomond in 1268 when he was killed in battle nearby, can be seen today in a specially created recess in the north wall of the chancel. It is marked by one of the few contemporary stone carvings of a Gaelic chieftain and honours the importance of the man and the debt owed to his family by the community at Corcomroe.

Wool production was an important element in the life of Cistercian monasteries and no doubt contributed to the economy of Corcomroe. However, the fourteenth century witnessed widespread disruption of the wool trade due to war, taxation and economic decline, and many Cistercian monasteries are known to have got themselves into debt through imprudent forward contracting during better times. Combined with declining population brought about by the Great European Famine of 1315–17 and the Black Death of 1348–50, this period represented a crisis for Corcomroe. Its precarious financial position was probably compounded by other disastrous dealings such as unauthorised leasing of property and sale of monastic assets. By the fifteenth century the congregation had declined to such an extent that the western part of the abbey was abandoned. A new dividing wall and west door were built. This wall included a bell tower, and the small opening in the arch of the door is the lower end of the chute that housed the rope that was used to ring the bell.

Contemplative retreat has always been part of the Cistercian ideal. Of necessity, this involves a large degree of self-sufficiency. As we have seen, Cistercians were accomplished masons and smiths, but they were also farmers, bakers, medics and brewers. Their skill as farmers is reflected in the Latin name that has long been associated with the abbey at Corcomroe – *Sancta Maria de Petra Fertilis* or 'Our Lady of the Fertile

Rock'. Though the modern townland of Glennamanagh [glan na manna] lies 4 km southwest of Corcomroe, the whole valley seems to have been referred to as *Gleann na Manaigh* [glown na monnig] or the 'Valley of the Monks' since the earlier occupation of the monastic settlement at Oughtmama on the opposite side of the valley to Corcomroe. The pattern of long rectangular fields surrounding both Corcomroe and Oughtmama can be clearly seen from Turlough Hill.

Perhaps the most interesting feature for the visitor to Corcomroe is the wealth of decorative stone carving to be found here. The high standard of functional masonry in the chancel and west wall was undoubtedly intended to honour the glory of God in traditional Cistercian fashion. The delicate carvings of flowers, 'dragons', human heads, chevrons and other devices tell a more personal story. It has been said that decorative carving was contrary to the Cistercian aesthetic tradition and that St Bernard in particular objected strongly to the practice as it distracted monks from their prayer. Neither claim is entirely accurate. There is a rich tradition of Cistercian decorative carving, especially of the capitals of columns where very intricate motifs can often be found. St Bernard objected to the subject matter rather than to the practice, denouncing as follies in his *Apologia* in 1125 'those unclean apes, those fierce lions, those monstrous centaurs, those half-men, those striped tigers, those fighting knights, those hunters winding their horns' that decorated the capitals in some cloisters.[11]

There are no such figures in the cloister at Corcomroe. Indeed, the only fantastic creatures here are the two 'dragons' carved on the outside corners at either side of the east window. Nevertheless, it is the subject matter that makes the capitals at Corcomroe entirely distinctive, and St Bernard himself might not have objected had he ever had the good fortune to visit the Burren. What more calming and restful image could the masons have carved and contemplated than the flowers with which they were familiar? It used to be thought that the flowers represented on the capitals at Corcomroe were a combination of native and imaginary species, but a detailed study by Nelson and Stalley shows otherwise, and in the process demonstrates that the masons at Corcomroe were well ahead of their time. Whilst some of the flowers cannot easily be identified and may therefore be imaginary, others are faithful representations of plants that the monks cultivated for medicinal and other purposes. Lily of the Valley, for example, represented on the northernmost capitals of the north transept, is not native to Ireland, but has been recognised at least since the Medieval period for its scent and medicinal properties. Not alone that, but its association with the Virgin Mary makes it particularly appropriate in an abbey dedicated to 'Our Lady of the Fertile Rock'.

Naturalism – the faithful representation of real objects – only began to exercise the minds of Medieval artists on the Continent in the early thirteenth century. Earlier art tended to be stylised, imaginative and often 'fantastic' – the focus of St Bernard's objections. Yet the masons at Corcomroe were already accomplished naturalist artists 'long before these artistic concerns reached Britain'.[12] Could French monks returning home from Ireland have brought the idea back with them?

Some of the carving on the capitals and elsewhere is very delicate and could not have been accomplished without the use of masonry drills. The Lily of the Valley referred to earlier is deeply undercut and unlikely to have been carved with a chisel alone. It is easy to imagine a mason drilling the holes under the bell-shaped flowers at the north end of the chancel arch. There can be little doubt that this technique was available to contemporary church masons; evidence for the use of drills can be seen on the capitals at the Benedictine abbey at Saint Benoit in France, for example, and early Cistercians are known to have recruited former Benedictine monks.[13]

Corcomroe's fate was sealed following the accession of Henry VIII to the throne and his subsequent troubles with Rome. The dissolution of the monasteries in the 1530s removed the great religious houses, their lands and assets from the ownership of the monastic orders. It is somewhat ironic, given the long association of Corcomroe with the O'Brien chieftains, that the abbey should have reverted in 1564 to Donnell O'Brien. This association was finally dissolved when possession of Corcomroc was given up in 1611 to Richard Harding. The Cistercians continued to worship here, however, until at least 1628, when Corcomroe was subject to the great abbey of Holycross in County Tipperary. It was from there that one John O'Dea was appointed abbot in that year. Unfortunately no information is recorded regarding the size of the community or for how long it survived after his appointment.

Muckinish Castles

Seanmuckinish
GR: M 2626 1038 Symbol:

Muckinish Nua
GR: M 2772 0919

The main interest for the visitor to the tower houses known as Muckinish is that they have both partially collapsed, opening a convenient cross-section by which to examine the construction of this type of building. There are similarities between the two, but also enough differences to provide a reasonably representative sample of the features and construction methods in use at the time they were built. The names derive from their construction dates, *sean* [shan] meaning old and *nua* [nooah] meaning new. Legend has it that they were built within three years of each other sometime in the fifteenth century.[14] *Muck inis* [inish] is an Irish language form for 'pig island'.

Both ruins reach almost to their full original height of just over 17 m and each includes the remains of two vaulted ceilings. Unfortunately neither of the staircases has survived. Good examples of intramural passages and stairs can be seen, especially at Seanmuckinish. Both include narrow defensive loops at lower levels and larger decorative windows in the top floor where defence was not an important design issue. The remains of bawn walls survive around both tower houses, that at Seanmuckinish in much better condition due to repair and maintenance in the eighteenth and nineteenth centuries.[15]

A much more pronounced base batter was used at Seanmuckinish and presumably incorporated loops in each wall although only three remain due to the collapse of the north wall. An additional loop was provided at the northeast corner at this level. Seanmuckinish is also distinctive for the internal wall rendering that can still be seen in some of the intramural passages and in the first floor reception room. That this was the principal room of the house is confirmed by the remains of a large stone fireplace in the west wall. It seems that the builders may have altered the plans in the course of construction as the fireplace is well tied directly inside a blocked window in the west wall. The large collapsed section of masonry to the seaward side of the ruin may include part of the chimney flue, and at least one decorated stone, possibly from the fireplace, can be seen among the rubble beside it. Muckinish Nua also had a fireplace, but the only visible evidence now is the flue that can be seen in some of the large sections of collapsed masonry.

The rectangular opening at ground floor level in the west wall at Muckinish Nua is the lower end of the garderobe chute that extended to the top floor. The garderobe chambers or privys, together with another small chamber can still be seen built into the west wall. An unusual opening through the west wall, like a short vent, leads from the arch over the ground floor loop, behind a floor level vent in the overhead privy, to a small, square external opening beside a vertical slit in the west wall. Its purpose is not clear and the vent in the privy may not be original, but it was undoubtedly constructed for a reason.

In general, Muckinish Nua appears to be the more refined of the two tower houses. The internal dressed quoins and arches show a greater concern for aesthetics than at Seanmuckinish, and remarkable attention to detail can be seen in the way the base of the ground floor loop in the west wall has been carved to allow drainage of water to the outside.

The remaining obvious difference between these two tower houses is the wall walk and machicolations at Seanmuckinish. Only the eastern and southern machicolations remain, but nineteenth-century drawings show that the small southern one was matched by similar examples on the west and north walls. The south machicolation, built roughly centrally in the south wall rests on three double corbels. Why it was considered necessary to build one here is a puzzle – it can scarcely have been required to defend the ground floor loop directly below. Perhaps it was the price to be paid for including a picture window in the fourth floor, though it seems inconceivable that this might have been a focus for attack.

The eastern machicolation is larger, resting on five double corbels and extending from the southeast corner to a projecting northeast corner. This corner housed the spiral stone staircase providing access to the living quarters and wall walk, and as we have seen it was defended at ground floor level with an additional arris loop.

Confusion caused by the similarity in the names means only vague details are known about the ownership and tenancy of the tower houses. Seanmuckinish was also known for a time as Ballynacragga Castle. After they were expelled from their family seat near Dromoland in 1654, the MacNamara family may have brought the name of their old castle with them when they settled at Seanmuckinish on the indented south shore of Galway Bay. The area was a haven for smugglers at the time due

Seanmuckinish Castle

to the duties levied on the export of Irish wool, and the MacNamaras of Ballynacragga probably participated in this activity.[16] Apart from the Ballynacragga period, the tower houses and lands were owned or occupied at various times up to the nineteenth century by members of the O'Loughlin, Neylon and Blake families.

Muckinish Nua Castle

Drumcreehy Church
GR: M 2474 0862

A low ridgeline stretching along the coast about 1.5 km east of Ballyvaghan was known in the Early Medieval period as *Droim Críche* [drim creeheh] and it is this ridge that has given its name to Drumcreehy church. The original name may have been *Droim Críche Uí Maille* [ee mawlyeh] (the ridge of O'Malley's territory) as it is thought to refer to the territory of the ancestors of the O'Malley family.[17]

Estimates for construction of the church that now stands on the ridge range from the eleventh and twelfth to the thirteenth or fourteenth century.[18] Though it was certainly in existence at the beginning of the fourteenth century when it was referred to in the taxation lists as Drumcruth, it probably consisted at that time only of the present collapsed nave, with the chancel added later, probably in the fifteenth or sixteenth century.[19] The walls of the original section, which have collapsed, are thicker than those of the chancel, which are still standing. The fine doorway in the north wall replaced the earlier door in the south wall of the nave.

Drumcreehy Church

A few hundred metres east of Drumcreehy church is an area known as Bishopsquarter. This was an area of land, probably about 120 acres (79 hectares) from which the Bishop of Kilfenora drew a monthly rent in the early seventeenth century. Whether or not he had a direct interest in the church is not recorded.

The remains of a shell midden can be seen outside the west end of the collapsed nave. It has not been dated, and so nothing is known about who may have dumped the oyster and other shells that continue to erode from the midden. However, it is known that oysters from Pooldoody Bay 2 km to the east were highly regarded in the nineteenth century. The oyster bed was owned in 1837 by J. S. Moran, and according to Lewis 'the oysters taken there have long been celebrated for their delicious flavour and are always disposed of by the proprietor in presents to his friends'.[20]

By 1842 the beds had come into the possession of a Mr Ryan, 'a gentleman no way churlish of its delicious produce who was obviously intent on preserving the reputation of Pooldoody oysters.'[21]

Gleninagh

Church GR: M 1933 1009	

Tower House and other monuments GR: M 1934 1032	

Gleninagh is the anglicised version of an original Irish name, usually taken to be *Gleann Eidhneach* [glown eyenock] meaning the ivied valley. The correct Irish name, however, may be *Cluain* [klooin] *Eidhneach,* the ivied retreat. The name certainly pre-dates the sixteenth century Gleninagh Castle that is the dominant archaeological feature in the area. Parishes are usually named after the principal church and this may be the case with Gleninagh parish.[22] The church, which is 250 m south of the castle, cannot accurately be dated without investigation, but it was certainly in existence in 1302 when taxation lists were drawn up. A monastic settlement called *Cluain Eidhneach* near Mountrath in County Laois that dates back at least to the eighth century was frequently referred to in the Annals of the Four Masters (e.g. AFM 767.4). Whilst there is no way now to be certain, the possibility that the present or an earlier church or monastic settlement in Gleninagh gave its name to the area should be borne in mind. Traditionally, however, Gleninagh is thought of as 'the ivied valley'.

Access to the church is by means of a pedestrian track off the R477. The road is narrow at this point and parking is very restricted. The road is also busy, especially during the summer. The other monuments described can be reached at the end of a narrow laneway marked on the map.

Church

The church is similar in many ways to other Medieval churches to be found in the Burren. It is rectangular, with a featureless north wall and narrow slit window in the east wall but no chancel. Though now in poor repair, it retains some of its early stonework and many of the features added later such as the pointed doorway in the reconstructed south wall. A possible arch springer lies in the graveyard. Cooke described a small altar with a recess underneath that contained at the time of his visit 'bleached bones, and other types of mortality'.[23] As parish churches go, it is on the small side, probably a reflection of the small population that it served. If seventeenth-century estimates can be extrapolated to preceding centuries, then Gleninagh was the smallest parish in the Diocese of Kilfenora in terms of population, and its survival is probably a result of the patronage of the owners of the nearby tower house.[24]

Gleninagh Church

Its origins may go back further than the fourteenth century, however, perhaps to an earlier monastic settlement. Outside the present churchyard wall, the outline of a possible enclosure can be traced in the field boundaries 30–70 m away. A curved field boundary, possibly a section of an outer enclosure, is marked on the 1842 Ordnance Survey map 150 m northwest of the church. Domestic waste uncovered near the church provides evidence of habitation, and there are traces of outbuildings in the graveyard near the east gable. Two neat rows of crude grave markers may point to early monastic burials. As it has not been investigated it is impossible to be sure of the date of the domestic waste material, but the middens at the settlement at Oughtmama provide an interesting parallel.

Incidentally, a small block of pink Galway granite in the graveyard attests to the tremendous power of the ice sheets that lifted it and many similar erratics and deposited them in the Burren as they retreated about 12,000 years ago.

Tower House
Gleninagh Castle was an O'Loughlin stronghold from the early sixteenth century, and though there were many changes of ownership over the following 300 years, it finally reverted to the family and was occupied by O'Loughlins until some time around 1840. It was described in 1839 as being 'in good repair and thatched with straw which gives it a rather

Gleninagh Castle

homely appearance'.[25] Cooke confirmed the thatched roof in 1843, but said that it was then being 'used as a barn by Mr. Blood, its proprietor'.

The building is unusual among Burren tower houses in that it is L-shaped in plan, the entrance and spiral stairs being housed off the southeast corner. Furthermore, the entrance is on the first floor and is accessed by means of a ramp. The heavy wooden door pivoted in the usual way on a hanging eye and spud-stone that can still be seen inside the doorway on the left. The entrance is protected by a machicolation built into the angle overhead. The other three corners are also protected by machicolations, in each case of uncommon circular design, and each with five musket holes. Wall openings are a mixture of loops and rectangular windows of various styles – mullioned and single light, hooded and plain. A second–third floor arris loop in the staircase defends the approach to the entrance. The tower house included garderobes at the northeast corner, and two waste chutes can be seen to the rear of the building.

The ground floor is a vaulted cellar with no windows and was accessed by means of a trapdoor in the floor above. The first floor was designed with defence in mind, with embrasured loops instead of windows in each wall. The second floor internal walls were plastered, which indicates, together with the large fireplace in the west wall, that this was the reception room. Gleninagh is similar to Seanmuckinish in this regard as both fireplaces required original windows to be blocked before they could be installed. Directly above, in the space beneath the vaulted ceiling, was a concealed room whose timber floor rested on corbels projecting from the north and south walls. It was accessed through a doorway above the garderobe. Loops in the east and west walls at this level, the only source of light in the chamber, were blocked sometime after construction. The third floor was refurbished, probably in the late sixteenth or early seventeenth century to provide more comfortable sleeping quarters. A double ogee-headed window in the north wall was blocked and replaced by a larger rectangular window to allow construction of a simple fireplace and chimney.

The roof must have presented an engineering challenge to the builders. It was built over four gables, two of which included chimney breasts. It may have covered a small attic room above the third floor as there are windows in the south and east gables. It is difficult to reconcile such a roof with what appears to be a wall walk unless the machicolations were abandoned when the roof was built.

Tower houses were protected from the weather by treating them with whitewash, a lime-based mixture that was brushed onto the external wall to provide some degree of waterproofing. The raw material – limestone – was obviously in plentiful supply in the Burren, but it needed to be prepared before application and part of the process involved firing crushed limestone in a kiln. The remains of one of these kilns can be seen beside the ringfort to the northeast of the tower house. A tall, newly whitewashed tower house would have made a striking statement about the status of the owner in Medieval times.

Ringforts

Two ringforts, one 120 m northeast of the church and another 60 m east of the tower house, confirm that the area has been inhabited since the Early Medieval period. The latter is the smaller of the two, but neither is easy to identify on the ground. The larger one is now bisected by a field boundary and almost obliterated by modern agriculture while the smaller one appears as nothing more than an undulating feature in the field to the east of the tower house.

The lime kiln mentioned above was previously thought to be a *fulacht fiadh* [fullokth feeah], a Bronze Age, open-air cooking site. There are *fulachta fiadh* nearby, however, indicating that the area was visited long before the more obvious archaeological remains were built.

Holy Well

A short distance south of the tower house is an elaborate holy well known over the years by a variety of names – Croghneva, *Tobar na Croise Naomhtha*

Gleninagh Holy Well

[thubber na krisslich nayfa], Tobernacrobaneede, Tobernacrohaneeve etc. Cooke states that it was dedicated to St Laurence, but this association is not reflected in any of the names recorded for the well.[26] The consensus is to refer to it as 'the well of the holy cross'.

The well is covered by a stone vault with a Gothic-style arched entrance. It includes a shelf that at the time of Cooke's visit was said to contain human skulls and round flat stones. It was at that time, and presumably for a long time beforehand, a place of pilgrimage. The tradition continues to this day (though the votive offerings are now somewhat less macabre) and the well is said to provide relief for eye ailments!

Gleninagh Lodge

The ruins of Gleninagh Lodge are worth noting even though, as a post-Medieval structure, they are not strictly of archaeological interest. They can be found at the end of the lane leading to the tower house. Though very little remains of the Lodge, mid-nineteenth-century maps show a number of large buildings and what must have been a very impressive formal garden immediately south of the holy well. Most of the land in the area was owned at the time by William Bindon Blood. The Blood family owned vast tracts of land in County Clare and counted among their illustrious ancestors one Colonel Thomas Blood (1618–80). Thomas had the distinction of being pardoned against all the odds by King Charles II following his attempt to steal the Crown jewels from the Tower of London in 1671.

Newtown Castle
GR: M 2171 0653

One of only three round tower houses to have been built in County Clare, Newtown Castle was restored in 1994 and is now part of the Burren College of Art. The tower house is open to the public and an account of the restoration works is on display within.

The political turmoil of the Medieval period makes it difficult, unless specific references are available, to establish construction dates and changes of ownership of tower houses. Though Newtown Castle is in the territory controlled by the O'Loughlins for much of the period up to the sixteenth century, it is said to have been built by the O'Briens, possibly in the last decade of that century.[27] A deed dated 9 June 1591 records the submission of the leaders of the O'Loughlin family to Donogh O'Brien, fourth Earl of Thomond, and contains references to O'Loughlin castles in the Ballyvaghan area, some of which had previously been 'occupied or plundered' by O'Brien.[28] Though no specific castle is named in this deed, Frost lists four castles in the area that were owned in 1580 by the O'Loughlins – Ballyvaghan, Seanmuckinish, Muckinish Nua and Newtown.[29] All eighteen castles in a 1584 list of castles in this area were owned by O'Loughlins. Newtown is not listed among them, nor was it included in the lists for 1570 and 1574. However, some of the castles named in the lists are no longer identifiable, and Newtown may be a later name for one of these.[30] The issue is further complicated by the fact that there is a second Newtown Castle in County Clare (near Parteen) and the records often do not distinguish between the two. Limited archaeological investigations in 1993–94 of the present Newtown Castle did not establish a definite construction date, but the fact that the third floor windows were glazed confirmed a late sixteenth or early seventeenth century date.[31]

The same archaeological investigations uncovered a lot of animal bone, teeth, flecks of charcoal, periwinkle, laser shell, oyster and the remains of a large area of cobbles near the castle. It was suggested that these might be evidence of a village that developed around the castle after it was built, perhaps the 'New Town' that gave its name to the castle. Much of the ground to the north of the castle where the animal and shellfish remains were found had been disturbed by the planting of an orchard that was marked on maps of the area in the early twentieth century. A section of wall across the road to the west of the castle may have been part of a bawn wall surrounding the tower house.

The tower house is very interesting from an architectural point of view. It is constructed over a square base on a plinth giving it a squat, solid appearance. Entry is through an off-centre pointed doorway in the east wall. A squint to the left of the doorway allowed those inside to see who was at the door before allowing entry. A small vaulted room to the right just inside the door was the gatekeeper's station. Despite the obvious concern for defence that these and other features demonstrate, the design of the building meant that it was not possible to include a murder-hole in the ceiling of the lobby. However, small holes in the spiral stairs may have allowed the occupants to defend against attackers ascending the stairs. One is above a small window at the ninth step and

Newtown Castle

the second is above the entrance to the main living quarters on the third floor. The steep batter of the base of the tower would have made it extremely difficult to get close to the building, and the loops at each apex provided those within with a means of using weapons to defend against any such attempt. Four machicolations staggered above the loops and a crenellated wall walk completed the exterior defensive measures.

The ground floor is vaulted and lit by a tiny north facing window. The vault was constructed by forming a domed wicker casing that was braced underneath with stout bent timbers set into notches in the wall. The stones that formed the vault were then laid in mortar over the casing, and when this had set and the vault was self-supporting the bracing timbers were removed. The remains of the vault casing and the notches in the wall can still be seen. Thick walls and limited ventilation ensured that this room remained cool and well suited to food storage.

The first floor had a timber ceiling (now reconstructed) supported on corbels, and is lit by four windows, each with circular gun loops on either side. It includes a large fireplace and wall niches and traces of wicker casing can be seen under the window arches. The second floor includes three slit gun loops alternating with two windows and what appears to be an external door. A vaulted ceiling was constructed in similar fashion to that above the ground floor.

The principal room of the tower house was on the third floor and was lit by four large glazed windows. The carved rebates and drilled slots used to secure the glass windows can still be seen. The room was warmed from a large fireplace and had a timber ceiling supported on corbels. The floor above, which was lit by four small rectangular windows, has been reconstructed as a mezzanine or gallery floor and houses an exhibition recording the reconstruction of the tower house in 1994.

Rathborney Churches

Rathborney
GR: M 2074 0474

Glenaraha
GR: M 2122 0498

These two churches are separated by about 500 m in the Rathborney river valley; both derive their names from local topography. Glenaraha is the anglicised version of *Gleann na Ratha* [glown na raha] (the Valley of the Raths/Ringforts) and one of these ringforts, known as Doontorpa, can be seen just to the east of Glenaraha church. Rathborney church was built on the site of another, *Rath Bhoirne* [raw vwirneh] (the Rath of the Burren).

Much of what remains of Rathborney church dates to the fifteenth century and represents an almost total rebuilding of the original, smaller church. Parts of the north and east walls are original. O'Donovan recorded a small belfry at the top of the west wall in 1839. The remaining fifteenth-century features include an elaborate east window and a smaller window set in an oblong internal recess in the south wall. The east window has a squared hood moulding over twin trefoil-headed lights on the outside and a large, plain, round arch inside. The doorway, also in the south wall, has a finely carved pointed arch. The jamb stones are no longer in place, but the hanging eye for the timber door can still be seen. Just inside the doorway is a corner stoup under a carved vault. A carved human head at the upper southwest corner of the church is part of a tradition of similar carvings to be found at many Medieval churches in the Burren.

As well as the modern gravestones in the cemetery at Rathborney, there are a number of crude grave markers that may be much older. Though it is difficult without further investigation to be certain, the presence of a bullaun stone in the cemetery, together with the fact that the original church was built before 1302 on the site of a ringfort would seem to point to a long, possibly monastic tradition here.

Glenaraha church is a large T-shaped church with a small vestry at the east end and another annexe at the west. It is modern and had a short lifespan. According to a plaque in the wall of the west annexe, it was built in 1795 – 'This Chapele was Built at The Sole Expense of The Most Noble the Marquis of Buckingham in The Year 1795 For The Advantage of His Tenants.'

George Nugent-Temple-Grenville (1753–1813), first Marquis of Buckingham, was twice Lord Lieutenant of Ireland and inherited the title Viscount Clare through his marriage to Lady Mary Nugent, daughter of the first Viscount. He owned large tracts of land in County Clare, but was an 'absentee landlord' and quite unpopular. His address at the opening of parliament in 1789 attracted the particular wrath of Henry Grattan who condemned 'the expensive genius of the Marquis of Buckingham in the management of public money'.[32] By 1837, the church building had been much enlarged, and a glebe of 40 acres had been allotted for the use of the parish priest.[33]

The Rath and Caher Mór

The Rath
GR: M 2242 0499

Caher Mór
GR: M 2200 0447

For the visitor interested in comparing different styles of ringfort, these two examples within 1 km of each other on the road (R480) leading south from Ballyvaghan are worth visiting. The Rath is a fine example of an earthen ringfort, with a deep external ditch and inner embankment. At the time of occupation, the ditch would have been deeper and the embankment higher and topped with a timber palisade. It is typical of the many thousands of earthen ringforts to be found throughout Ireland. Caher Mór is a reasonably typical 'cashel' or stone fort, at least in terms of siting and size. What is slightly unusual is the elaborate entrance flanked by guard chambers, and this may indicate that it was occupied by a high status family group. The entrance was constructed some time after the original cashel was built and may reflect an improvement in the fortunes of the original occupants, or possibly later re-occupation by a different group. Among the artefacts recovered during limited excavation and reconstruction of the entrance in the late 1990s was a coin dating from 1690. This does not necessarily indicate occupation of the cashel at this date, but seventeenth-century occupation of ringforts and cashels is not unknown. For a general description of ringforts, see the section on the Early Medieval period in Chapter 1.

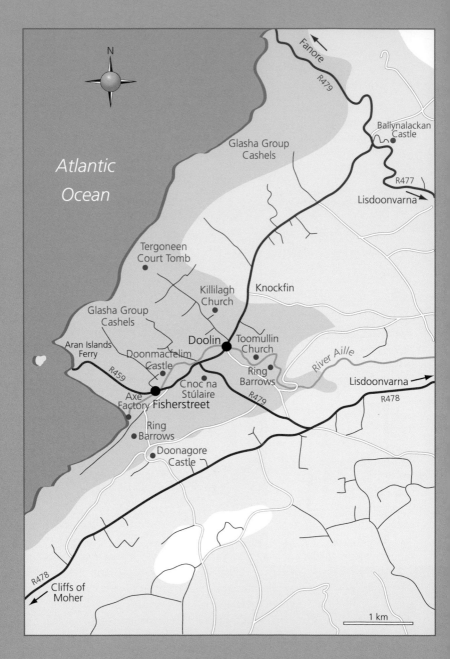

Burren West

4. Burren West

Doonagore Castle
GR: R 0687 9569

Doonagore Castle is one of three tower houses in the Burren to have
been built to a circular plan; the others are Newtown and Faunarooska.
The original 'castle' may have been a fourteenth-century structure built
by Teigue MacTurlough MacCon O'Connor; this in turn might have
been built on the site of an earlier ringfort (possibly the original *dún*
of Doonagore) located a short distance away. O'Donovan referred in
1839 to 'a doon on the summit of a small green hill in the Townland of
Doonagore' that had by that time been completely effaced. Westropp
later referred to a caher near the round castle of which only a trace
of the northern segment remained. The present tower house probably
dates to the middle of the sixteenth century.

Most, if not all, of the built heritage of the Burren is of limestone
construction. Doonagore Castle, on the other hand, is constructed of
sandstone, the use of this material simply reflecting the underlying
geology. The stone used in the construction of Doonagore was extracted
from a quarry known as *Trá Leachain* [thraw lacken] about 2 km to the
southwest. (*Trá Leachain* means 'flaggy beach', flag referring in this case
to the flagstones quarried there.) Some of the decorative architectural
features of the tower house are of finely carved limestone.

The tower house consisted of four floors over a cellar with a stone
beehive vault between first and second floors. The entrance doorway to
the northeast was protected by a machicolation accessed from the wall
walk. The tower was surrounded by a bawn wall. An unusual and possibly
unique feature can be seen on close examination of the garderobe chute
in the southeast section of the tower that is outside the present bawn
wall. Four stone projections, one at each corner of the lower opening,
are grooved 'as if to let down a cover from above'.[1] The purpose of such
a cover must be a matter for speculation, but it may be connected with
the smaller opening above the main chute, which is also unusual. It can
hardly have been a defensive feature; it could easily be dismantled from
outside and there is no trace of a machicolation above. In any event,
the usual method of preventing access through garderobe chutes was to

Doonagore Castle

insert a metal grille internally across the shaft. On the other hand, since garderobes were smelly places, especially when ammonia was used as a disinfectant, this installation may have been an experimental way of controlling airflow through the shaft to prevent odours from reaching the living quarters above. We may never know the original intention, and for the moment at least, one guess is as good as the next.

Doonagore has had many different owners since it was first built. It was certainly in existence by 1570 when it was owned by Sir Donnell O'Brien. Brian MacCahill O'Connor was recorded as the owner in 1582. By this time, however, the fortunes of the O'Connors were in decline and wholesale transfer of land and property was in progress in the area. The records may reflect landlord/tenant/occupier relationships rather than straightforward ownership. In 1583, much of the land and property in the area was formally surrendered to the Crown and re-granted to Turlough O'Brien of Ennistymon as head of the O'Brien clan. Doonagore then came into the possession of the Mc Clancy family, the hereditary brehons to the O'Briens of Thomond. Following the rebellion of 1641 the Cromwellian settlement saw Doonagore granted to John Sarsfield.

By unfortunate coincidence, ownership of Doonagore passed some time around the end of the seventeenth or beginning of the eighteenth century to the Gore family, leading to the erroneous belief that the name means 'Gore's castle'. In fact, the name is derived from the Irish *Dún na Gabhair* [doon na gore] and means the fort of the goats, or possibly of the rounded hills. The Gore family repaired the tower house during their tenure in the early part of the nineteenth century, but by 1837 it had again fallen into disrepair. For a more detailed discussion of the ownership of Doonagore, see Breen and Ua Cróinín, 2002, pp. 8–10.

The present restoration was completed in the 1970s following purchase in 1971 as a private residence.

Ring Barrows
GR: R 0661 9608

Accurate dating of the Doolin ring barrows will require formal investigation, but evidence from elsewhere would suggest that they probably date to the Iron Age. A ring barrow is a low mound of earth surrounded by a ditch and an external bank of earth. Most are between 15–25 m in diameter and they are often found in groups. Many ring barrows have been damaged or destroyed during cultivation of the land in recent times. The Doolin ring barrows are typical in all these respects.

One group can be seen to the east of the dirt track leading towards the Cliffs of Moher at GR: R 0661 9608, and another to the east of *Cnoc na Stúlaire* [knuk na stoolera] (Stoolery Hill) at GR: R 0825 9680. There are other, isolated, barrows. One at GR: R 0982 9782 is known as *Cnocán na Crocaire* [knukawn na krukareh] and is said to be the location for the mass hanging of sailors of the Spanish Armada who were unfortunate enough to have been forced to come ashore during a storm in September 1588. A *cnocán* is a small hill, and *crocaire* can mean a traitor, a villain or a hangman. Further east along the road to Lisdoonvarna at GR: R 1160 9799 is another isolated ring barrow. All these ring barrows are on private property.

An interesting feature of some ring barrows found elsewhere in Ireland is their association with standing stones – tall slender stones probably used in this case as markers to identify the location of individual barrows or cemeteries.

Doolin 'Axe factory'
GR: R 0652 9647

At the beginning of the twentieth century, antiquarians began to note and record finds of shale flakes at the mouth of the River Aille at Fisherstreet near Doolin that appeared to have been worked into the shape of crude tools such as axes and scrapers. It has not yet been possible to date the Fisherstreet tools accurately. Nevertheless, it is certain that the hinterland was a focus for human activity at least from early Neolithic times. The court tomb at Teergonean demonstrates that there was a settled community living in the area at that time. Earlier, more mobile Mesolithic hunter-gatherer communities favoured river mouths for their seasonal base camps and such a group may well have foraged and fished back along the river towards Lisdoonvarna using the thousands of cobbles at the mouth of the river as a source for their tools.

Further erosion of the sandhill at the mouth of the river will probably produce more evidence for an 'axe factory'. More useful, however, may be similar erosion of shell middens or dumps along the high-water line where food waste such as oyster, mussel, periwinkle and other seashells as well as animal bones may be unearthed. A group of stray finds discovered in Doolin in 2000 includes an interesting polished stone axe that is believed to have been manufactured in Cumbria in England. It is the only one of its kind to have been discovered in County Clare and points to an extensive Neolithic trade network. These and many other artefacts can be seen in the Clare County Museum in Ennis.

Doonmacfelim Castle
GR: R 0711 9691

The few extant references to Doonmacfelim are very brief and for the most part simply record ownership, tenancy and transfers of both at various points in time. The fact that the word *dún* is included in the

Doonmacfelim Castle

title may indicate that there was an earlier fort or stronghold at the site, probably in the form of a substantial cashel or ringfort as at the neighbouring Doonagore Castle. If there was a fort here, it may have belonged to a son of one of the Felim O'Connors listed in the Annals during the thirteenth, fourteenth and fifteenth centuries, long before the present tower house was built. The tower house dates to the end of the fifteenth or the beginning of the sixteenth century and is believed to have been an O'Connor property. It passed into O'Brien hands in 1584-85 when every head or chief of a sept in the Barony of Corcomroe was deprived of title and tribute.[2] By the middle of the seventeenth century it had been transferred following the Cromwellian Settlement to a John Fitzgerald.

Cnoc na Stúlaire
GR: R 0763 9686

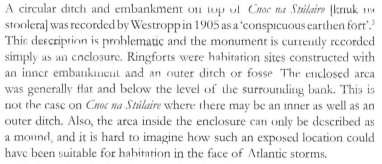

A circular ditch and embankment on top of *Cnoc na Stúlaire* [knuk na stoolera] was recorded by Westropp in 1905 as a 'conspicuous earthen fort'.[3] This description is problematic and the monument is currently recorded simply as an enclosure. Ringforts were habitation sites constructed with an inner embankment and an outer ditch or fosse. The enclosed area was generally flat and below the level of the surrounding bank. This is not the case on *Cnoc na Stúlaire* where there may be an inner as well as an outer ditch. Also, the area inside the enclosure can only be described as a mound, and it is hard to imagine how such an exposed location could have been suitable for habitation in the face of Atlantic storms.

It is unclear in the absence of archaeological investigation whether the two standing stones within the monument (one of which has fallen) were placed at the time it was originally constructed or were added later. There have been suggestions that the stone still standing may have been an ogham stone, but this has been generally discounted since Westropp's time, any hint of ogham script being nothing more than natural weathering. The stone is an obvious marker, perhaps for a burial, a tribal inauguration site or something else that has long since disappeared from our collective consciousness.

Toomullin Church
GR: R 0835 9709

Toomullin church was in use at the same time as its near neighbour at Killilagh. Traditionally, it is believed to have been founded by St Brecan, the fifth-century disciple of St Patrick who is credited with bringing Christianity to the region from his monastery on Inis Mór, the largest of the Aran Islands. It is mentioned in taxation lists at the beginning of the fourteenth century, and this has been interpreted as an indication that it was then a parish church. However, if Toomullin was a parish, it was soon subsumed into the larger parish of Killilagh and disappeared from the record. In the taxation lists of 1302–06 it was one of the two poorest churches in the Diocese of Kilfenora. Considering that it was located in a well populated area, and that Killilagh was one of the wealthiest churches in the diocese, its function is all the more puzzling. Ironically, the very wealth of the locality may help to resolve the puzzle.

The church was originally much smaller than it appears today, and if it was founded by St Brecan it was certainly a timber structure. At some point, a small stone church was built and subsequently modified during the Medieval period. Living quarters on two floors were incorporated at the west end. The ground floor of these quarters consisted of two rooms and was accessed from inside the church through an arched doorway with a hanging timber door. The first floor was supported on six corbels. The builders had an eye for symmetry when arranging these corbels, with three of curved profile and three of diamond profile arranged in alternating pairs on opposite walls. This floor may also have consisted of two rooms, but since the west end of the south wall has collapsed it is difficult to tell if it included a window to light a separate room. The window opening in the north wall included an outward opening timber shutter (the eye and pivot stones are still in position). Access from the main body of the church to the first floor was by means of a timber stairs and a landing supported on two corbels in the dividing wall. Another arched doorway gave access to the living quarters and this also retains its original eye and pivot.

While residential quarters are not unknown in Irish Medieval churches, the clearly defined apartment at Toomullin is unique in the Burren. The church is only a short distance from the site of Toomullin Castle, the tower house residence in the mid-sixteenth century of the Mc Clancy family. As we have seen, the Mc Clancy family was one of the leading families in west Clare in the Medieval period, and the small church beside their castle may well have benefited from their patronage. Again, this was not uncommon in Medieval Ireland. Some tower houses included their own internal chapels and it would seem reasonable to suppose that the pre-existing church of Toomullin might have served as the family chapel in this case.

Most of the south wall has collapsed, but some interesting features remain. The east wall retains a fifteenth-century single-light, ogee-headed window with carved spandrels and a moulded hood superimposed over the base of a larger early window. The frame consists of punch-dressed stone, and the whole was neatly inserted into the original wall. The original church appears to have had two opposing entrances in the north and south walls near the west end of the church, but whether they were in contemporaneous use is unclear. The west gable wall was topped by a small belfry before the extension was built, and a new pointed doorway had to be inserted to provide access to the extension.[4]

In 1941, a bronze brooch dating from AD 200–300 was found in the graveyard of the church. Unfortunately, the graveyard, the tomb of Conogher Mc Clancy and St Brecan's holy well no longer survive.

Toomullin Castle
GR: R 0823 9716

Toomullin Castle, which was for a long time the residence of the Mc Clancy or MacGlanchy family, hereditary brehons of Thomond, is another monument in a ruinous state. Brehons were the interpreters and administrators of the Medieval Irish legal system known as Brehon Law, and in this capacity the Mc Clancys were privileged and respected members of society. Their original seat appears to have been the cashel known a Cahermaclancy, not far from Ballynalackan Castle. Famed for their legal expertise, they were awarded freehold possession of substantial tracts of land and property in west Clare; their law school was located on the site of the present-day Catholic church at Knockfin crossroads, 1.5 km north of Doolin. Mc Clancy brehons are recorded at least as far back as the middle of the fifteenth century and their descendants were prominent in the area until the middle of the seventeenth century.

Conogher Mc Clancy and Hugh Mc Clancy are recorded as owners of Toomullin Castle in the middle of the fifteenth century and Hugh's direct descendant Boetius owned Knockfin Castle, just to the north of the law school, in 1580. Knockfin and Toomullin Castles and the law school were all intervisible. Doonagore Castle was also in Mc Clancy hands for a period from c. 1589.

Unfortunately for the Mc Clancy family, their reputation was tarnished when Boetius Mc Clancy, in his role as Sheriff of County Clare, ordered and supervised the hanging of sailors of the Spanish Armada who sought shelter from a storm in September 1588. Not content with hanging the sailors, he had the bodies thrown in a mass grave and had a large table made from some of the timber salvaged from one of the shipwrecks. Many years later this table was presented to Conor and Máire Rua O'Brien, owners of Leamaneh Castle. The table has been preserved and can now be seen in Bunratty Castle. Very little is known about the tower house apart from scant ownership records. It was built on the steep north bank of the River Aille within sight of Toomullin church. It is now almost completely destroyed and the only remaining feature of note is a section of the circular staircase. This had steeply battered walls and was supported on a specially constructed base on the river bank.

Killilagh Church
GR: R 0779 9777

Killilagh is a large parish church with side chapel, which was extensively reconstructed around the fifteenth century. It is one of the few Medieval churches in the Diocese of Kilfenora to have a side chapel. Killilagh was one of the wealthiest and most populous parishes in the Burren throughout the Medieval period and included the fertile strip of land between Doolin and Ballynalackan. This area was known as *Tuath Glae* [thua glay], and these were the hereditary lands of the Mc Clancy family that were held free of rent due to the family's high status as Brehon lawyers.

The original church was built before the fourteenth century but not much remains of the fabric of this building since it has been extensively remodeled. It is this remodeling that provides the interest today, with fine fifteenth-century stonework to be seen in the windows and on the arch between the church and side chapel. Unfortunately, some of this stonework is in imminent danger of collapse. Indeed much damage has already been sustained with the east lancet window destroyed when the gable wall was blown over in a storm in 1903. The square belfry on top of the west gable has also been damaged and is in precarious condition. A carved stone head, familiar from many other Burren monuments, lay in the graveyard for many years before disappearing in 1971. It has since been recovered and can now be seen at the Burren Centre in Kilfenora. The north door was blocked up during reconstruction, and an unusual stone in the jamb of the new south door has been interpreted as a reused bullaun stone. It would have been laid flat in use, the saucer-shaped depression containing holy water. The mausoleum to the south of the church was built as a MacNamara family vault, but remains unused.

Two other monuments can be seen near the church – the faint remains of a ringfort in a field to the east, and a mound immediately to the west of the church that is probably one of the many ring barrows that were used for burial in the Iron Age.

Killilagh Church

Teergonean Court Tomb
GR: R 0685 9847

We are fortunate to have a few examples of court tombs in the Burren – the distribution of this monument type is overwhelmingly in the northern third of the country. It was originally believed that the court tomb builders arrived in Ireland across a land bridge linking the northeast of Ireland with Scotland. It now seems more likely that they arrived by sea (from where is a mystery) and that their earliest settlements were in the area of north County Mayo and Sligo Bay. They appear to have migrated inland and along the coasts to north and south. If distribution is an accurate reflection of the migration pattern, then court tomb builders arrived in the Burren late in the sequence, possibly 3500–3000 BC. Support for this pattern is provided by recent excavations at a local variant of the court tomb type at Parknabinnia where this date range has been confirmed by radiocarbon analysis.[5]

The court tomb at Teergonean is in a poor state of repair and it is difficult to see the layout or to distinguish the characteristic court at the northeast end of the burial chamber. A few upright stones forming a fragmentary arc are all that remains of the façade. The cairn of stones that originally covered the burial chamber has long since disappeared.

Incidentally, the monument gets its name from the townland in which it is located – Teergonean. This is an Anglicised version of an original Irish name, but the exact form of the original is unclear. It is often reverse-translated today as *Tír gan Éan* [teer gone ayn], probably following Frost's list of Clare place names.[6] He translated this as 'the birdless district', which is indeed the literal translation of *Tír gan Éan*. This translation and re-translation seem contrived, however. Westropp suggested that the name derives from one of three cashels in the townland 'nearly levelled before 1878; one may have been the Caherguinine of the records'.[7] But he also managed to extract at least three other forms of the name from old records – Tregownine, Tirgounine and Tirgearnine.[8] All of which does nothing more than raise another question – who or what was 'guinine', at which point the investigation runs into the sand.

Teergonan Court Tomb

A section of the Glasha Group of cashels and ancient field walls
(courtesy Ordnance Survey Ireland)

The Glasha Group

The narrow strip of limestone on the coast between Doolin and Ballynalackan is a maze of cashels, enclosures and ancient field systems that bear witness to centuries of human habitation and intensive farming. The distinction between cashel and enclosure is blurred in the Burren – if enclosures were primarily animal pens, then cashels often fulfilled the same requirement in addition to being farmsteads. The Glasha group (named after two townlands between Doolin and Ballynalackan) consists of fifty or more of these cashels/enclosures, and, strictly speaking, should include the associated field systems, since they are an essential part of the infrastructure of the community that farmed the area in Early Medieval times and later. The field systems can best be appreciated from aerial photographs, where modern field boundaries can be seen superimposed over a patchwork of low mound walls that are sometimes difficult to distinguish on the ground. The cashels varied in size and quality of construction, reflecting the status of the occupants. Undoubtedly one of the most important was Cahermaclancy. Located on the highest point of the Glasha ridge towards the northern end of the group, it was the seat of the Mc Clancy family, hereditary lawyers to the Earls of Thomond.

It is worth noting the different forms of the ringforts in the Doolin area. The Glasha Group is near the shoreline on the west side of the road between Doolin and Ballynalackan; these are cashels, or stone forts. To the east of the road in Toomullin and Gortaclob is a group of earthen ringforts. This is a direct result of the underlying geology, the land to the east being generally fertile soil over shallow boundary layers of shale, in contrast to the thin soil over the coastal limestone strip.

Ballynalackan
GR: M 1037 0032

Given its commanding position, it is hard to imagine that the site of Ballynalackan Castle was not occupied since the Early Medieval period. However, any evidence for such an occupation (which, if it existed at all, would have been in the form of a cashel) has been obliterated by construction and modification of the tower house that now stands on the bluff overlooking the coastal lowlands north of Doolin. If there was a cashel on the site, it would almost certainly have been occupied from the tenth century by a branch of the O'Connor clan, rulers of West Corcomroe. The name is an anglicisation of *Baile na Leachan* [bolyeh na lackan], which probably means the town of the flagstones, the tombstones or simply the stones – appropriate, given its position at the edge of the Burren. An alternative Irish language origin may be *Béal Áth na Leachan* [bail aw na lackan] (the ford-mouth of the flagstones), which would be a reference to a ford across the stream running in the gorge below the tower house.

Lochlan MacCon O'Connor is believed to have built a fortress here towards the end of the fourteenth century. The form of the fortress is not recorded and it may simply have been a stronger version of a previous cashel. In any event, it is extremely unlikely to have been an early version of the present structure; tower houses are unknown in Ireland before the fifteenth century, and the Burren in particular was insulated from this Anglo-Norman-inspired building style until much later.

The present tower house is a multi-period structure, similar in many ways to Leamaneh Castle. The earlier phase consisted of the tall, slender eastern tower. Whilst the intention for this phase was to provide basic accommodation and strong defence, the plan seems to have been to improve the property fairly quickly afterwards. External doorways were included to allow for access to the more spacious and comfortable accommodation built subsequently.[9] The slit windows of the early tower are similar to those of Leamaneh Castle, indicating a construction date towards the end of the fifteenth century.

The O'Connors lost control of their territory in 1564 and ownership of Ballynalackan was formally ceded to Sir Turlough O'Brien in 1584–85. Turlough's son, Daniel, was obliged to petition in 1654 (successfully) to save it from destruction by the English Commissioners following the Irish Rebellion of 1641 and the subsequent Cromwellian conquest. At the time of his petition to Colonel Stubber in Loughrea, he described 'a little castle which is already demolished by the Irish, by name Ballenalacken which hath no bawn or Barbican that stands as yet'.[10] It is not clear whether he meant that the bawn and barbican had been destroyed or had not yet been built; the remains of both, as well as a postern at the northeast corner of the bawn, can be seen at the castle today. Daniel's intention seems to have been to build substantial houses here and at Dough near Lahinch, and it is likely that he or his son, Teige, eventually undertook construction of the extension that can be seen at Ballynalackan today. Teige's son, Donough, seems to have been the first of the O'Briens to describe himself as 'of Ballyneleackan'.[11]

The extension at Ballynalackan is more compact and not nearly as elegant as that at Leamaneh, consisting as it does of a mixture of single-, double- and triple-light windows with round and square heads. Nonetheless, there is symmetry to the layout, with the largest windows opposed and lighting the best room or rooms at the top west corners.

Two machicolations, on the north and west walls, are no less puzzling than a counterpart at Leamaneh Castle, which as we have seen is similar in many ways to Ballynalackan. Whereas defensive machicolations are commonly built over doorways or at corners and are accessible from the wall walk, these two are not of classic form, though each is provided with musket holes. They could both be used to provide defence in depth to the gatehouse in the bawn wall. This was located in the western wall, although the doorway and four overhead corbels that supported the barbican are all that remains of the structure today. The fact that the machicolations in the main building are internal structures projecting from the principal rooms of the later accommodation wing indicates that they may have had a domestic as well as defensive purpose. As at Leamaneh Castle, they may have been en suite privys, though in the case of Ballynalackan an intramural garderobe was built at first floor level in the south wall. By contrast, the earlier machicolation on the east wall is clearly defensive, built as it is with wide floor openings directly over the main entrance.

Ballynalackan Castle continued in use as a residence of the Ennistymon branch of the O'Brien family until around the middle of the eighteenth century when it became the property of a different branch of the family.

Ballynalackan Castle

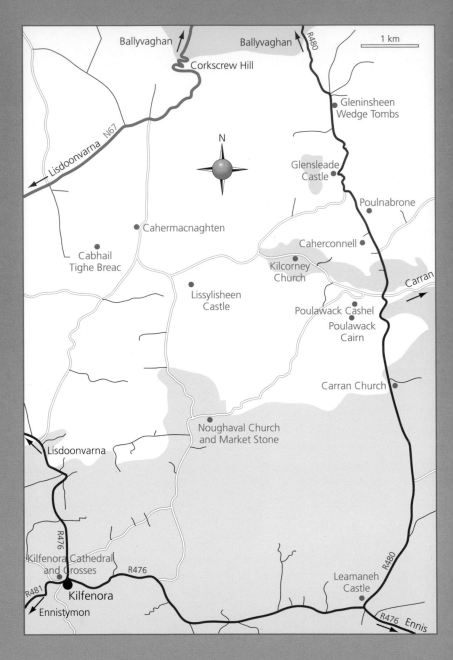

Burren Central

5. Burren Central

Leamaneh Castle

GR: R 2348 9357

Situated at one of the most important road junctions in the Burren, Leamaneh Castle is probably the most familiar, and one of the most photographed monuments in the area. It is no coincidence that it should be located at such an important junction, as many of the modern roads follow ancient routes and pathways that linked the settlements, chiefdoms and ecclesiastical sites to which the lives of the people who have lived in the Burren for millennia were so intimately bound.

The Burren is divided in two by a natural route running north-south between Ballyvaghan and Leamanch. In prehistoric times, this route is believed to have been used for access to the Burren uplands, and the portal tombs or dolmens at Poulnabrone and Ballycasheen may have been a type of territorial marker proclaiming the territory of a contemporary tribal group.[1] The southern limits of the Burren are defined roughly by the modern road that runs east-west from Corrofin through Leamaneh and Lisdoonvarna to the coast near Ballynalackan.

The area now known as the Burren consists of two baronies, Burren to the east and Corcomroe to the west. By the fifteenth century, the O'Briens had more or less established their authority over the Barony of Inchiquin (south of the Burren) and Corcomroe. Despite their encroachment and influence, however, the Barony of Burren remained an O'Loughlin stronghold. Leamaneh Castle was built by the O'Briens about 1480 right at the junction of the three territories in an attempt to extend and consolidate their influence over the entire region.

Though the site is not accessible today due to the poor state of repair of the building, much is known of its history. The original building was a tower house – the tall, slender, eastern section of the building that we see today. It was one of the early Gaelic tower houses, characterised by narrow window slits known as 'arrow loops'. Two of these are built into the southeastern and northeastern angles of the tower about halfway up the building, and are known as 'arris loops'. This initial phase of building may have been completed quickly simply in order to secure the site, the intention being to continue later with more spacious quarters. Similar intent is in evidence at Ballynalackan Castle, another O'Brien tower house, where the original slender tower house was subsequently extended to include much more spacious accommodation.[2]

The tower house at Leamaneh was built c. 1480–90 by Turlough Donn O'Brien who died in 1528. It was occupied by four following generations until it came into the possession of Turlough's great-great-great grandson Conor, who was born in 1617. By this time, the O'Briens had become firmly established in the Anglo-Irish aristocracy, Conor's father Sir Donogh O'Brien having been knighted by King Charles I. The lords and ladies of this new aristocracy consolidated their status through marriage, and it was thus that Conor came to marry Mary, daughter of Sir Turlough MacMahon in 1639. This is the Máire Rua [mawreh rooah] (red-haired Mary) of legend, and stories abound of her deeds and misdeeds, mistreatment of husbands and servants, prowess in battle and ruthlessness. Much of what has been said of her is legend, but she does seem to have been energetic, single-minded and slightly cold and calculating. By virtue of a previous marriage, Máire was in receipt of a substantial income from the estate of her eldest son who was at that time still a minor, and it is likely that it was this income that permitted her and her new husband to undertake, in 1643, a significant expansion of the family home at Leamaneh. Comfort and an ostentatious display of wealth and status seem to have motivated the expansion. A magnificent four-storey manor house was added to the original tower house, increasing the accommodation at least four-fold. An architectural *trompe d'oeil* was used to distort the already impressive proportions of the building; the size of the windows was reduced with each storey to give an exaggerated impression of height.

A second-storey machicolation at the southwest corner is curious. It includes what appear to be musket-holes, indicating a defensive purpose. However, if the times were considered peaceful enough to build a stately house with large ground-floor windows, it is difficult to understand why such an elaborate defensive measure was considered necessary, and why at one corner only (the northwest corner is equipped with a simple embrasure with an arris loop). It was designed as an internal structure, roofed with stone tiles and accessed from a large corner room through an unusual corner doorway that was not at floor level. In addition to being a defensive structure, it may have served a secondary function, perhaps as an en suite privy that could be used for defence when required. The similarity with machicolations at Ballynalackan Castle is striking.

A bawn wall surrounding the extended building included an elaborate arched gateway erected in 1643. This stood opposite the entrance door of the manor house until 1906 when 'Dr G. Macnamara … on December ninth, found several men engaged in demolishing the outstanding porch'.[3] They were acting on the instructions of Lord Inchiquin, who had arranged to have it re-erected at Dromoland Castle, which had by then become the chief residence of the Leamaneh branch of the family. It can still be seen today in the garden of Dromoland Castle Hotel.

The manor house and bawn were not the only projects to have been undertaken at Leamaneh, though Conor did not live to see them all completed and may not even have had anything to do with some of them. He was killed in battle in 1651, defending his territory against the advance of a Cromwellian army led by General Edmund Ludlow who was born, coincidentally, in the same year as Conor. Ludlow is the man who famously said of the Burren that it was a place where there was 'not enough water to drown a man, wood enough to hang one, nor earth enough to bury him'.

Leamaneh Castle

Conor's death left Máire with a problem. Because of his tactical error in opposing Ludlow, there was a real danger that his estate would be confiscated. To neutralise this threat, Máire married a junior officer, Cornet John Cooper, who was based in Limerick in General Ireton's garrison. Cooper continued the successful management of the estate and may have been responsible for some of the later developments at Leamaneh.

A large garden to the east of the building was enclosed by a turreted wall and included a wall walk, a 'garden temple' or gazebo and a large linear fish-pond. Traces of these can be seen in the fields to the southeast of the modern road leading to Ballyvaghan. The hill to the southeast of the garden was also enclosed and became a deer park. Conor and Máire's son Donough (also known as Donat), born in 1642 and dispatched to London to study as a goldsmith, eventually recovered the estate in the family name and set about expanding O'Brien hegemony over large parts of County Clare. By 1678, the Leamaneh estate included well over 10,000 acres of land.[4] A determined businessman, Donough avoided the extravagant expenditure of his father. Rather, his projects were investments intended to provide financial return. The modern road between Killinaboy and Leamaneh is known as Sir Donat's Road, and its flanking stone walls can still be seen. It was a toll road, furnished with gatehouses (which have since been demolished) at which travellers through the estate were required to pay taxes. Donough transferred the O'Brien seat to Dromoland in 1684, and before his death in 1717 he had consolidated the family's position with various honours and appointments. He was knighted in 1686, served as Sheriff of Clare in 1690 and was Member of Parliament for Clare between 1695 and 1713.

An original fireplace from Leamaneh can be seen in The Old Ground Hotel in Ennis.

Carran Church
GR: R 2340 9738

Traditionally known as the parish church of Carran, this was referred to as 'Karne Ch.' on a map drawn in 1787 by Henry Pelham, an American cartographer, and as 'Kearne' on *Hiberniae Delineatio,* a map of Ireland engraved c. 1663 for Sir William Petty, an Englishman tasked with completing the Down Survey following the Cromwellian conquest.

Many of the architectural features of the church indicate a fifteenth-century date for construction, but it may have been built slightly earlier than that. It is of simple rectangular plan with no chancel. Despite the simple plan, the church has a number of unusual features.

Perhaps the most obvious is the stone feature high up at the northwest corner of the building. In his *A Folklore Survey of County Clare,* Westropp recorded the tradition that: 'The northwest corner of Carran church overhangs, and is destined to fall on the wisest man that shall pass underneath.' In a previous publication he had described it as a machicolation.[5] Whilst machicolations are often built as defensive features, especially in tower houses and castles, this example probably had a different function. Some clues as to its purpose can be found inside the west end of the building. A series of corbels and window frames above the doors on the north and south walls show that there was originally a room overhead. This would not have been unusual at the time and it was probably the living quarters of a resident clergyman. This is a domestic arrangement, therefore, and the structure at the corner is simply a waste chute serving the clergyman's private quarters. A thin stone slab fixed under the opening and angled out from the wall was an attempt to prevent the waste from soiling the wall, which would have been whitewashed in use. This slab was dislodged by frost during the severe winter of 2009–10.

The remains of a bell chamber can be seen in the west gable of the church. The north wall is featureless except for a blocked entrance opposite the present south door. Until recently the inside north wall included three intriguing carved heads, only one of which remains. It can be found at about waist height towards the east end of the church. Westropp suggested that these three carvings may have been corbels, but this is highly unlikely given their original position low down at the eastern end of the north wall and that they would be unsuitable for supporting beams. Carvings of a crowned man and a woman with elaborate head-dress were removed in the 1970s. The remaining carving is of a man wearing either a type of helmet known as a basinet or the padded hood or coif worn under such a helmet. The style is typical of the late fourteenth and early fifteenth centuries, the basinet having developed by then from the original form worn under the cylindrical 'great helm' used typically by the Crusaders of preceding centuries. Later basinets were often fitted with a chain mail cowl – known as an *aventail* – to protect the shoulders. The cowl was attached to the helmet using metal eyes known as *vervelles,* and this carving includes rows of holes drilled along the front edge of

Carran Church

the helmet to represent the holes through which the *vervelles* were fitted.

Westropp included Carran among a group of churches where 'nearly complete rebuilding was effected during the fifteenth and early sixteenth century'.[6] Typical fifteenth-century architecture to be seen here includes diagonal tooling and moulded carving at the door and windows, particularly the ogee-headed window near the east end of the south wall. However, as the gaps between the finely carved stone of the inserted door and the wall are filled with spall, it seems safe to assume that the door was inserted into an existing wall when the previous north door was blocked rather than included in a complete rebuild. Similar spalling can be seen around the windows in the south wall. The doorway also includes evidence of repair; a small cut stone has been inserted to restore the inner angle of the jamb. Beside this repair, a cross has been inscribed on the jamb. The inscribed cross is unusual, though not unique. It is not a consecration cross as these come in groups of twelve, referring to the Twelve Apostles. It may simply be a local adaptation or tradition. A reused stone can be seen in the inner face of the south wall, above and to the left of the doorway. It is semi-circular in shape, with a cutout at the bottom. Westropp described it as a broken quern stone, but in fact it is the head of a narrow slit window, splayed on the inside and similar to those found in the oldest stone churches such as Templecronan and Oughtmama.[7] Here again, the intention of the builders is unclear, but since the walls of the church would have been plastered and possibly whitewashed or painted in use, this stone would have been hidden. A stoup for holy water built into the door jamb is similar to others found in churches in the Burren. Also built into the doorway are slots (one long and one short) for the drawbar that would have been used to secure the door from the inside. When not in use, the drawbar was withdrawn and stowed in the longer slot. Curiously, these slots are not aligned. The hanging eye on which the door was pivoted is still in position. A hanging eye of a different sort, in this case to pivot a timber shutter, can be seen in the inserted cross member of the east window.

The name of the parish, of which this is the principal church, may be derived from the Irish word *carn* [karn]. This might refer to the cairn to the southwest of the church, though O'Donovan discounted this possibility.[8] The cairn has not been excavated, but tradition suggests that it was a form of station around which coffins were carried prior to burial. The more likely origin for the name is the Irish word *carran*, which like *boireann* means 'rocky land'.[9] The graveyard around the church is more extensive than is suggested by the visible evidence and was shown to be larger on old maps. It includes many simple early grave markers and there are the remains of small buildings to the north and northwest of the church.

Poulawack Cairn and Cashel

Cairn
GR: R 2324 9853

Cashel
GR: R 2333 9874

Great care is required when accessing these monuments. The terrain is difficult and should only be attempted with suitable footwear by those who feel fully confident traversing rough ground. It is easy to get disoriented on the featureless plateau, and careful note should be made of the access route to facilitate safe return.

The small cashel is almost completely demolished but includes a chamber in the remaining northern section of the wall. This is accessed from within the cashel by means of a short passage. Intramural chambers were occasionally built into cashel walls, but these cashels tended to be much more substantial than this one. This chamber may have been added or built after the cashel had been abandoned as a habitation site.

The cairn of stones that sits atop the plateau to the south of the cashel is unimpressive at first sight and reveals nothing of its long and complicated history. It is about 21 m in diameter and only 2.5 m high, but on excavation it was found to contain the remains of sixteen people in numerous discrete burials of various types.

Poulawack was first excavated in 1934 by Dr Hugh Hencken of Harvard University and has since then been the subject of many further investigations. Hencken's initial interpretation of a two-phase construction over a relatively short period in the Early Bronze Age (2000–1500 BC) has been superseded, and it is now clear that the cairn was constructed in three phases over a period of about 1,800 years.

Phase I, a polygonal cist (a box made with stone slabs), dates to about 3350 BC, placing it firmly in the Neolithic, so it was in use around the same time as Poulnabrone portal tomb. The cist contained the remains

Poulawack Cairn

of three adults and a child as well as some other objects, and it appears to have been covered by a low cairn of stones with a surrounding circle of kerbstones 10 m in diameter.

It was over 1,000 years before the second phase of construction took place, when three more burial cists were inserted into the original cairn, which had by then probably partially collapsed over the retaining kerbstones. The remains of eight individuals have been associated with this phase and dated to around 2000 BC, although the burials may have taken place over a number of generations.

The final phase of construction happened over a relatively short period between 1600–1400 BC, when the original cairn was covered by a new, larger cairn, with a new enclosing circle of kerbstones about 14 m in diameter. Three further cists were inserted containing the remains of three individuals. The crouched remains of another individual were found to have been placed on the original surface of the plateau, covered with slabs, and then covered by the expanded cairn.

There is a continuity about Poulawack that can be contrasted with the different prehistoric burial types found elsewhere in the Burren. Whereas portal, court and wedge tombs seem to represent different traditions spanning relatively discrete periods from the Early Neolithic to the Early Bronze Age, burials at Poulawack continued throughout the same period with slight variation in form. Why should this be so? Does it suggest a different ethnic group living in the area alongside those represented by the other burial traditions? Or does it suggest a burial type with a distinct ritual purpose that continued to be important while other traditions changed during this period?[10] Like many questions in archaeology, this one will have to wait until new evidence becomes available.

Kilcorney Church
GR: R 2246 9955

Kilcorney church lies in a small, quiet valley to the west of the modern road between Leamaneh and Ballyvaghan. Two other churches are also found here, though their history and interrelation are a bit of a puzzle. Kilcorney church is the main structure to the south of the road. Nothing is known of its founder, and claims referring to a St Coirné seem to be invention, since no such saint is recorded and no other reference to a person of that name has been unearthed. It is unclear, therefore, what the second part of the place name is derived from. It is possible, but this is purely speculative, that the name may have something to do with a monastic tradition at the site.

The remains of Kilcolmanbara (the church of Colman Báire) lie 350 m to the west of the present church. Very little is known about this church. It may still have been in use in 1675 when a reference to a tract of land known as *Cille Cholmáin Bháire* [killeh kulmawn hawreh] was included in a deed drawn up by Hugh and Cosny O'Davoren in the nearby law school at Cahermacnaghten. The church is now barely discernable, and it had been abandoned by 1839 when neither the church nor the tract of land was referred to in the 'Name Book of Kilcoarney'.[11] However, two nearby monuments also bear Colman's name; Liscolman is a cashel on the hill just above Kilcolmanbara, and a holy well dedicated to St Colman *(Tobar Cholmáin Bháire)* is located about 1.5 km to the north. At least three St Colmans are known from the Burren and all are associated with monastic sites.

Between Colman's well and the present Kilcorney church is another holy well, *Tobar Inghine Bhaoith* [thubber ineena vwee]. *Inghine Bhaoith* is also associated with a type of early convent at Killinaboy. A third holy well, *Tobar na nAingeal* [thubber na nangle] (the well of the angels), is located by the roadside 160 m east of the church. The two holy wells to the north of the church are in direct line on an approach route from that direction that descends to the valley through a natural pass in the limestone terrace; *Tobar na nAingeal* is on the approach from the east. Given the association between holy wells and pilgrimage, it seems reasonable to assume that the original church, Kilcolmanbara, may have been a focus for pilgrimage, possibly as far back as the Early Medieval period.

The Irish word *coirneach* [kwirnock] means 'tonsured' or 'a tonsured person'. It would not be too far-fetched to see this as a reference to monks who may have settled and built their church in the quiet valley of Kilcorney. In this case, *Cill Coirneach* (Kilcorney) was the original 'church of the monks'. There is also a possibility that the 'Chapel of the Monks' recorded in fourteenth-century taxation lists is not, in fact, Corcomroe as suggested by Westropp, but rather Kilcolmanbara/Kilcorney. If it were Corcomroe, its very low valuation in contemporary taxation lists would be anomalous whereas a connection with Kilcolmanbara/Kilcorney would be more plausible.[12] As noted, however, this is speculative and must await further study.

Incidentally, in the tradition of holy wells in Ireland, both *Tobar na nAingeal* and *Tobar Cholmáin Bháire* are associated with cures for eye ailments, and *Tobar Inghine Bhaoith* with a cure for warts.

The present church of Kilcorney is co-located with another church or chapel, the remains of which can be seen at the west end of the main church. Westropp dated some of the features of Kilcorney church to the eleventh or twelfth century and its old masonry, some of which is cyclopean, probably to the tenth century.[13] Nothing is known of the co-located chapel, nor of its relationship, if any, with Kilcolmanbara. The three may even have been in use at the same time, each fulfilling a different function within a monastic settlement similar to those at Oughtmama. In any event, the present church continued to be developed for some time after it was first built. A decorated Romanesque window head and a fragment of a fine Gothic south doorway can be seen in the grounds of the church.

The parish of Kilcorney was in existence in 1302, presumably with this as the parish church. It was the smallest parish in the Diocese of Kilfenora and could therefore be expected to have been the poorest in terms of church income. This is borne out by the record, Kilcorney ranking twenty-first of twenty-three in the taxation list of 1302–06.[14] However, despite the small size of the parish, the church is in the medium range in terms of size and is slightly unusual in having a chancel. This indicates that Kilcorney benefited in some way from the support of a powerful patron. The Bishop of Kilfenora, newly elevated following the church reforms of the thirteenth century, may have chosen to patronise a nearby monastic settlement. It is more likely, however, that

Kilcorney Church – carved window head in church grounds

the O'Loughlin chieftains of the Burren, owners of nearby Caherconnell cashel and of Glensleade and Lissylisheen tower houses (all less than 2 km from Kilcorney) were the patrons.[15] In the latter case, the small attached chapel could have been a proprietary or a mortuary chapel of the O'Loughlins.

The only interesting features to be seen at Kilcorney today, apart from the remaining structure of the church and chapel, are the carved stones scattered in the graveyard, a baptismal font on its plinth inside the south door and the occasional dressed stone in the graveyard wall.

Directly to the south of the church is an area of low ground that, depending on the time of year and recent weather conditions, may be flooded. The flood rises and falls through a cave in the cliff face known as the 'Cave of the Wild Horses'. Legend has it that at certain times wild horses rushed out of the cave to breed and that their descendants could be found in the area. This legend was obviously related to Westropp who recorded: 'I have heard locally strange stories of the untameable recklessness and savage temper of alleged descendants of the fairy horses.'[16]

Another legend tells of an enchanted bird with the voice of a human that lives in the cave. The legends have their origins in the sounds that come from the cave when water flows with force into the valley. Lewis describes how it is 'occasionally spouted into the air to a great height'.[17] Yet another legend, again described by Westropp, tells that in the eighteenth century the cave was famous for throwing out floods of water full of fish. No doubt he was disappointed by the inconvenient fact that 'the floods have been rare and insignificant since 1833.'

Caherconnell
GR: R 2361 9949

Cashels generally range in size from 20–25 m in diameter. Caherconnell is unusually large at 40 m. The walls of the cashel currently stand to about 3 m in height but were probably 4 m high when in use. Impressive proportions such as these would suggest that it was built and occupied by an important family, and this indeed seems to have been the case. As luck would have it, Caherconnell and its immediate vicinity have been the focus of a series of archaeological investigation that started in 2007, and these are continuing to reveal something of the history and context of the community that lived here. Excavation reports are published regularly by Comber and Hull, and the most recent information regarding the cashel and satellite sites produced here is derived from these reports. Caherconnell now includes a Visitor Centre with an audio-visual display and cafe.

Long before the cashel was built, Neolithic or Early Bronze Age people built a rectangular timber structure in a hollow just to the southwest. The postholes from this structure were discovered during investigation of a small adjacent stone building in a deeper section of the hollow. This appears to be unique in Ireland and Britain and is still being analysed. It may have been a Medieval corn-drying kiln, but the partial remains of three people found dumped at the entrance and dating to the fifteenth or sixteenth century are unexplained.

One of the most important contextual aspects of Caherconnell is that it is located in an area that remained insulated to a greater or lesser degree from the influence of Vikings and Anglo-Normans. East Corcomroe was an area controlled in the early centuries of the second millennium AD by the O'Loughlin family. The O'Loughlins seem to have been fiercely independent, resisting complete submission to the powerful, Anglo-centric O'Briens until the early seventeenth century. Caherconnell was built sometime between the early tenth and mid-twelfth centuries. This was a time when the tradition of building and living in cashels and their earthen counterparts (raths) was declining elsewhere in Ireland, a

Caherconnell – recently excavated entrance and internal path

decline that accelerated following the arrival of the urbanising Anglo-Normans.[18] It is not unique in this regard, but it is quite unusual.

The occupants of Caherconnell maintained the traditional way of life insofar as they could in the face of modernising pressures all around them. It is not clear if the cashel was occupied continually during the tenure of the O'Loughlins. It may have been abandoned for a period corresponding with the widespread economic decline in the fourteenth century, but by the late fifteenth or early sixteenth century the builders were back at work, this time to construct a small rectangular house, the outline of which can be seen in the northern part of the cashel, and possibly some of the other structures that can be seen in and around the cashel. On this occasion, the occupants may have been a minor branch of the family, the senior former occupiers having built and decamped to Glensleade Castle about 3 km to the north. The rectangular house is similar to many others recorded elsewhere in Ireland that were used as dwellings by mid-ranking families. Some were built within existing cashels, for example at nearby Cahermacnaghten and Caher Mór, and others were built outside. Westropp recorded external side-posts in the cashel wall in 1899, and investigations in 2010 uncovered an elaborate early entrance and a paved path with kerbs leading into the cashel.[19] No sketch or photograph of the entrance exists so it is impossible to be sure of its form, but it may have been similar to examples at Cahermacnaghten and Caher Mór. Caherconnell shares another characteristic with these two cashels, in that its ground level has been raised by the accumulation of occupation debris over the centuries.

By the sixteenth century the English influence had become overwhelming, East Corcomroe was now the Barony of Burren. Those who embraced the English way of life were rewarded with official favour and status and those who did not were systematically excluded. The O'Loughlin mini-hegemony was dismantled, and though they continued to style themselves 'Kings of Burren' even into the nineteenth century, the fact was that by the seventeenth century their halcyon days were over. It is not known when Caherconnell was finally abandoned, but it appears unlikely that it continued in use as a residence much beyond the end of the seventeenth century.

Perhaps one of Caherconnel's greatest legacies is that it allows us to speculate on how Gaelic society might have developed were it not for the influence of the Vikings in the ninth century and the Anglo-Normans post-1169. Would ringforts have continued to be used as the predominant form of settlement among high-status landowners? Would the trend towards urbanisation have been postponed? Would we have been better insulated from the devastation of the fourteenth century? If not, and left to our own devices, how would we have responded to and exploited the economic recovery of the fifteenth century? Hypothetical questions certainly, but worth considering nonetheless.

Poulnabrone Portal Tomb

GR: M 2361 0037

The impressive portal tomb at Poulnabrone is one of the most accessible and most photographed ancient monuments in the Burren and, indeed, in the country. It stands in a prominent location near one of the highest points in the Burren landscape and is now believed to mark an access route into one of the 'tribal' homelands of the Neolithic period.

Poulnabrone was excavated in 1986 and 1988 following the discovery that one of the stones forming one side of the tomb was cracked and in danger of collapsing the tomb. The remains of thirty-three individuals were found, men and women, adults and children, as well as various objects of stone and bone. The human remains were dated to the period 3800–3200 BC. A number of interesting things were noted about them:

- There were no intact skeletons. The bones were randomly jumbled together, which indicates that the tomb was not used in the usual sense of a grave where a body is placed immediately after death.

- Later bones were found beneath older ones, indicating that they were not buried sequentially.

- Only one of the people buried at Poulnabrone appears to have lived beyond forty years of age.

- The bones of many of the adults showed evidence of arthritis in the upper torso.

- The teeth of the children showed evidence of illness or malnutrition.

- A skull and a rib bone had depressed fractures that had healed before death.

Poulnabrone Portal Tomb

- An adult male hip bone had the tip of a stone projectile (possibly an arrowhead) still embedded in it. This injury had not healed, and therefore occurred at or about the time of death.

What does all this evidence suggest? It would appear that the structure had a ritual or ceremonial purpose, possibly announcing the limit of a territory that lay to the south in the Burren uplands. The lowlands were covered by dense forest at the time, and it is clear from other archaeological evidence that the uplands were the focus of extensive agricultural and settlement activity in the Neolithic.

Nobody knows what criteria were used to decide which remains were placed here, but clearly some few were chosen while others were not. It seems reasonable to assume that they were some sort of elite or that they were considered to be important ancestors. After death, the bodies were left, apparently somewhere safe, to decompose. There is some evidence from elsewhere in Ireland that bodies were left exposed to the elements and scavenging animals after death before being formally interred, but no such evidence is available from the remains at Poulnabrone. No cut- or tooth-marks were found on any of the bones, which included many small examples that would have been carried off by animals and birds had the bodies been left exposed to the elements. Indeed, scorch marks that were inflicted on some of the bones after they had dried out indicate that they may have been removed from their original safe burials and purified by fire in some ritual way before finally being laid to rest at Poulnabrone.

One further body was discovered at Poulnabrone near the front of the tomb. It was that of a newborn baby dating to the Early Bronze Age between 1750–1420 BC.

Gleninsheen Wedge Tombs
GR: M 2298 0216

A roadside field between Caher Mór and Poulnabrone demonstrates perfectly the richness of the archaeological heritage of the Burren. Within an area of a few hundred square metres, three items spanning the Bronze Age have been identified.

The Gleninsheen Gorget (see photo on p. 14) is a superb example of a type of gold ceremonial neck or collar ornament made and worn among the upper echelons of society around 800–700 BC. It was found in 1932 by a local man, Paddy Nolan, concealed (and probably folded in half) in one of the many grykes or cracks in the field. It is now on display in the National Museum of Ireland in Dublin.

Not far from where the gorget was found are the remains of two wedge tombs dating from the end of the Neolithic or beginning of the Bronze Age. One is visible just inside the road wall on the east side of the road, and the other, which is partially collapsed, can be seen about 100 m to the northeast in the middle of the field. As with all wedge tombs in Ireland, both these are aligned with the wider, open end facing towards the setting sun. These are only two of the many wedge tombs to be found in the Burren.

Gleninsheen Wedge Tombs

Cahermacnaghten

Cashel	
GR: M 1967 0011	

Law School	
GR: R 1891 9971	

Cahermacnaghten has long been recognised as the ancestral seat of the O'Davorens, a prominent Burren family. The O'Davorens were brehons or legal advisers to the O'Loughlins, who styled themselves 'Kings of Burren' during the Medieval period, and it was long thought that the famous O'Davoren Brehon Law school was based in the cashel. It now appears that, while the cashel was certainly the family residence, the law school was probably housed in another building located 870 m to the southwest known as *Cabhail Tighe Breac* [kowil chee brack].

The O'Davorens were known as legal experts in the fourteenth century, and probably for some time before that – Brehon Law dates back at least to the third or fourth century AD. The Annals of Connaught record the death of *Gilla na naem Duib da Boireann* [O'Davoren] in 1364, describing him as a Brehon Law *ollamh* [ullav], a term translated today as 'professor'.[20]

The cashel was occupied at least until the seventeenth century. A surviving deed of 1606 formalises the division of the property between two sons of Giolla *na naomh óg* O'Davoren, so presumably it was occupied for a time after this division. This late occupation accounts for a few notable features of the cashel.

- The accumulation of occupation debris probably accounts for the fact that the present floor level is considerably higher than the surrounding ground level. The rising floor level probably necessitated raising and repairing the cashel wall, and evidence for this can be seen in a line of levellers, or thin stones laid on the flat at various points around the wall.

- A cluster of five rectangular stone buildings can be identified within the cashel, each of which is mentioned in the aforementioned deed.

Cahermacnaghten – remains of cashel entrance

- The remains of an elaborate, two-storey, fifteenth-century entrance or gatehouse have replaced the entrance passage more usually associated with cashels. Unfortunately, the gatehouse has collapsed, but some of its grandeur can be imagined from nineteenth- and early twentieth-century descriptions and photographs, at least one of which shows the hanging eye on which the strong wooden door was hinged still in place.

The O'Davoren deed also describes the division of the lands and infrastructure immediately surrounding the cashel. This area was known as the *ceann áit* [keawn awtch], or principal place of the O'Davorens, and was, in turn, part of a wider community centered on Cahermacnaghten. At least four other cashels, together with numerous enclosures and a mosaic of field walls stretch about 3 km along the shallow valley running northeast-southwest through Cahermacnaghten. These may not all have been O'Davoren lands, but there can be little doubt that the area was home to a large community and that it was more densely populated in the sixteenth and seventeenth centuries than it is today.

Cabhail Tighe Brew has been the subject of ongoing archaeological investigation since 2007. It is a single-storey, three-roomed stone building with a loft overhead that seems to have been purpose-built at the turn of the sixteenth century as an institutional space. As if to confirm the building's use as a school, a fragment of slate with a single inscribed character was found during recent excavation. It is similar to slates and fragments that have been found throughout Europe at Medieval school sites.[21]

Noughaval Church
GR: R 2083 9674

There are three church buildings at Noughaval, as well as the remains of a settlement, a holy well and a market stone. The modern building dates to 1941. It was originally located in Ballyvaghan where it was used by the Church of Ireland congregation. It was bought for £25, dismantled and transported by truck to Noughaval where it was reassembled and rededicated in 1943 as a Catholic church.[22] The Second World War had necessitated the introduction of food and fuel rationing in 1941, and it is believed that a special dispensation had to be obtained to allow for refuelling of the trucks used to transport the dismantled church.

Like many Medieval churches in the Burren, Noughaval has been repaired and modified since it was first built, probably in the Early Medieval period. The original building may have been the core of a monastic settlement, represented by the cluster of field walls and outlines of stone buildings to the south of the church. Certainly, the masonry style of the nave is early; the later chancel consisted of smaller, roughly coursed stones. The traditional patron or supposed founder is an obscure figure, and the name by which he is now known – St Mogua – may be a corruption of another, possibly St Colman Mac Duagh. In any event, the holy well to the east of the church is known as St Mogua's Well, and it lies in the shadow of an ash thicket. A previous ash tree collapsed before 1896, whereupon 'the fragments rooted and grew up into considerable trees'.[23] That there was a large population living in the area immediately surrounding the church and stretching for some distance to the southeast is beyond doubt. Westropp describes 'a group of forts so numerous and implying so much labour that we may conclude that an actual city and considerable population occupied this lonely site'.[24] The name of the ecclesiastical site derives from the Irish name for 'new settlement' – *Nua Chongbhail* [nuah howawl].[25] When, exactly, the settlement could have been described as 'new' is unclear, but it may have been around the beginning of the fourteenth century.

The west gable of the church had been destroyed by the early nineteenth century, but probably included an original lintelled doorway. This was replaced in the late twelfth or early thirteenth century by the present south doorway. The pointed arch of this doorway includes finely carved chevron ornaments of a type introduced into Ireland around the middle of the twelfth century. Similar ornamentation can be found in the vault and on a sedilia at Corcomroe Abbey and on decorated arches elsewhere in Clare and Galway. They are characteristic of the architectural style known as the School of the West, and the same masons may well have worked at both Noughaval and Corcomroe. The lintel was inserted later still; it is hard to imagine that the masons would work so diligently on the voussoirs only to obscure their handiwork with the rough stones now in the tympanum (the space between lintel and arch).

The insertion of the new south doorway was probably part of an extensive reconstruction that also included the addition of the chancel and chancel arch as well as some or all of the windows in the south wall. One of these (immediately west of the chancel arch) is unusual among

Burren churches, being of an oblong, mullioned form more usually seen in domestic buildings.

The small chapel beside the Medieval church is a mortuary chapel of the O'Davoren family – interpreters of Brehon Law, legal advisors to the O'Loughlin chieftains of the Burren and operators of the law school at Cahermacnaghten. It had a vaulted roof, only part of which remains. Also missing are the pointed south door and an inscribed stone described in 1839 by O'Donovan in his Ordnance Survey Letters. The stone commemorated the construction (or repair, if Westropp is to be believed) of the chapel by James O'Davoren who died in 1725.

Immediately to the west of the mortuary chapel is a *leacht* or outdoor altar with a weathered stone cross in the style of a ringed high cross. The presence of a *leacht* at the site indicates that Noughaval was a place of pilgrimage in the Early Medieval period.

Part of the shaft of a market stone stands at the entrance to the old church. The shaft is octagonal and stands on a stepped base – a typical configuration for such structures. It is sometimes referred to as a 'market cross', and though one of the most important Irish high crosses (in Kells, County Meath) is known as the 'Market Cross', this one is from an entirely different tradition. Very little is known of the origins of the Noughaval 'market cross', but we may speculate on its origins and function by reference to others from the same tradition.

Market crosses are widespread in Britain, dating as far back as the thirteenth century, and are particularly associated with Scotland, where they are often referred to as 'mercat crosses'. To refer to these as crosses is misleading, however. The 'cross' in this case refers to the square or crossroads where the market was held, rather than the stone or timber pillar associated with the market. Various types of market were thus identified, and towns often had a market stone for each market. Melton Mowbray in Leicestershire, for example, had Sheep, Corn, Butter, Beast and Sage Markets, four of which are known to have been marked by market stones. Their prominent central location meant that they often became associated with other events and rituals not directly connected with the marketplace such as public meetings, payment of secular and church taxes and reading of marriage banns. To this day, the calling of Scottish general elections and the succession of monarchs are still announced at the Mercat Cross on Edinburgh's Royal Mile. Whether the Noughaval market stone can validly be associated with any particular aspect of the British market or mercat cross tradition is open to question. It may, indeed, have taken on a purely local character and use that is now lost to posterity.

Noughaval market stone

Kilfenora
GR: R 1833 9400

In 1979, during the visit of Pope John Paul II to Ireland, a group of parishioners from Kilfenora made the journey to Phoenix Park in Dublin to attend an open-air Mass celebrated by the Pontiff. They carried a banner with them which read 'Our Bishop, our Pope'. What a wealth of history was evoked by this simple message.

Kilfenora became a diocese of the Catholic Church in AD 1152 at the Synod of Kells, having failed to be recognised as such at the earlier Synod of Rathbreasail in 1111. The site had ecclesiastical connections going back possibly to the sixth century, when St Fachtnan is believed to have founded a monastery there. Whatever about its origins, the imprint of the monastic site can still be seen in the layout of the village, the main street of which curves along the southern boundary of the ancient termon. A holy well dedicated to St Fachtnan can be found at the end of the lane running north of the cathedral.

The focus of the site today is the cathedral building and the remaining 'High Crosses'. The high crosses at Kilfenora constitute the largest collection of such objects from a single site in Ireland. They date to the latest phase of the monastic settlement when it may have been a centre for production of such crosses. At least seven are known, five of which are housed in the cathedral at Kilfenora; one appears to have been lost or destroyed and another was removed in the eighteenth century and is currently in St Flannan's Cathedral in Killaloe.

The Doorty Cross
The Doorty Cross is so named because the lower section of the shaft used to mark a Doorty family plot in the cemetery where it was placed upside down over the grave. The inverted commemorative inscription can now be seen at the bottom of the shaft. It was reunited with the upper part of the cross in 1955. The whole is almost completely covered with carving, not all of which is fully understood.

On one face are three groups, probably related. Uppermost is a figure with his head centered on the cross ring wearing a conical mitre and a long robe with a decorated collar. The ears are prominent, and on his shoulders sit two winged creatures that may represent birds or angels. His left hand holds a crozier with a spiral head and his right, formed in a traditional Christian symbol of benediction, is extended downwards, possibly indicating the figures below. The crozier is one of three carved on this face of the cross. Immediately below the mitered figure, two others with interlinked arms hold two different styles of crozier. The figure on the right, which is hooded, holds a long staff with a Tau head. The crozier held by the figure on the left has a traditional Irish form of crook head. The pointed ends of both croziers appear to be piercing a winged creature underneath, which in turn appears to be devouring or pecking at one of two human heads.

There has been much speculation regarding this group of carvings, most of which suggests that they refer to the reorganisation of the Church in the early twelfth century as an episcopal hierarchy.

The opposite face of the cross includes two groups. The uppermost is a badly weathered figure also with prominent ears, apparently with arms outstretched along the arms of the cross. In this case, the chest is centered on the cross ring, and four birds, each inturned, occupy the quadrants. The only other part of the figure that can be distinguished is the lower left leg and foot, which is shown in profile.

Beneath this is an elaborate interlace, one end of which seems to be held by a human figure. The figure is accompanied by a horse or donkey and the two are carved above a shingle roof. The symbolism here is even more obscure than that of the opposite face. The upper figure is too weathered to permit interpretation, and it is not clear, as has been suggested, that it represents Christ crucified. The four birds arranged around the figure are also open to interpretation. The shingle roof at the base of the shaft is not unlike those seen on some surviving 'house shrines'. These were ornamented containers used around the end of the first millennium to store important relics for safe keeping and while being transported on pilgrimage. Whether the figures above are spatially related to the shingle roof is unclear; the latter may be an independent element, similar to that at the base of the West Cross described below. The interlace above the figures has elements of contemporary Scandinavian styles.

The narrow sides of the Doorty Cross include carvings of two further robed human figures, poorly executed, and three panels with geometric designs.

The West Cross

Situated in a field about 200 m to the west of the cathedral, the West

Cross is the tallest and most elaborately decorated of the high crosses at Kilfenora. On the west face, the cross, ring and upper part of the shaft are decorated with very elaborate interlace, ropework and geometric panels, including an unusual interlocking design on the lowest panel. At the base of the shaft is a triangle with an interlace knot motif.

The opposite face includes a human figure with arms outstretched and surmounted by a small, stylised animal figure. The ring and the upper part of the shaft include finely decorated geometric and interlace panels. The human figure carries a large, square object suspended from his neck by a crossed string or cord. He stands on a ropework triangle, and the ropework extends to another triangle at the base of the shaft. This plain lower triangle may be unfinished, or it may be a template for the gable end of a small tent-shaped shrine. The latter interpretation would fit with the tradition of pilgrimage associated with Kilfenora. Tent-shaped shrines were used to house relics that pilgrims venerated and often touched on their rounds.

The South Cross
The lower section of the shaft is all that remains of the South Cross. The upper parts of both faces are decorated with interlace panels and the angles of the shaft are decorated with roll mouldings extending to spirals at the base.

The North Cross Fragment
This cross is unringed and, in its present form at least, much shorter than the others. The decoration is also less intricate, though one face does include interlace patterns at the top. The most interesting feature is a domed boss at the intersection of the arms and shaft. Bosses are not uncommon on high crosses; they are often smaller than this example and can be found on ringed crosses where the ring intersects the arms and shaft. They are believed to be a legacy of a time when high crosses were made of timber when the joints may have been reinforced or secured with dowels.

Cross Fragment
A section of the tapering shaft is all that now remains of the last surviving cross. It is finely decorated on both faces, one in circular motifs with roll moulded edges and the other in predominantly angular motifs.

Cathedral

The cathedral is multi-period and a curious mix of styles. In common with many early ecclesiastical sites in Ireland, the original church may have been a timber structure; it was certainly so if founded in the sixth century. There is no visible evidence today of such a structure, however. The oldest part of the stone building seems to be the north wall of the nave that was constructed in the cyclopean style common to churches built towards the end of the first millennium. The nave, including the cyclopean north wall, is today protected from the elements by plaster as this section of the building is still used by the Church of Ireland community of the area. It may originally have been aisled.[26]

The chancel of the Medieval cathedral dates to the late twelfth or early thirteenth century and reflects the importance of the building following the creation of the new Diocese of Kilfenora in 1152. It includes elements of a style of architecture known as the 'School of the West' that was in vogue in the west of Ireland in the early thirteenth century. The decorated east window, with its three lights surrounded by a moulded frame, is typical of this style and is similar to the east and west windows at Corcomroe Abbey, which was built around the same time. Also reminiscent of Corcomroe, though stylistically quite different, are the decorated capitals above the mullions of this window. A matwork pattern can be seen in the plaster of the large arch above the three window lights. It is not uncommon to find similar patterns in Medieval churches and tower houses. Flexible mats were used to centre and form arches during construction. When the arch was completed, the mats were removed leaving the pattern imprinted in the plasterwork. The outermost roll moulding of this arch is terminated at each end by a carved bird pecking at a bunch of grapes.

There was undoubtedly a lot of remodelling over the course of the first three centuries of the cathedral's existence, and at least some of the decorative stonework appears to have been taken from other buildings for reuse in the cathedral. The north wing includes two windows in round-headed Romanesque style and one window, two doors and twin arches in pointed Gothic style. A small wall niche with two arches is also Gothic; it may originally have included a dividing colonette, but this no longer survives. There is no discernable plan or pattern to these features. One of the Romanesque windows has a sill that is similar to another under a later wall plaque in the chancel. It is likely that these were taken from elsewhere and inserted into the fabric of the cathedral building. Indeed, a similar sill can be seen under a commemorative plaque in the church at Killinaboy. Corbels can still be seen in the north wing indicating that it originally had two storeys, and the windows and twin arches post-date the removal of the upper storey. The recesses in the west wall of this wing may be putlog holes, in which case this wall was probably built at a different time to the others.

There are fifteenth-century modifications and additions in the chancel; two windows and a door in the south wall of the chancel include typical Gothic tracery decoration with interesting stylised animals carved on some of the finials. A triple-arch niche in the north wall is decorated in late Gothic style and centered above this niche is a fourteenth-century carved mitered head. A similar carved head can be found above the entrance to the church at the southwest corner of the building. The chancel also includes a number of seventeenth-century grave slabs, one of which was inserted in the south wall.

Three interesting carved slabs in contrasting styles have been removed for protection from the elements to the entrance hallway of the church. One consists of an incised effigy of a bishop holding an Irish style crook headed crozier. Another bishop is represented in a deep-relief carving framed by a Gothic arch. He wears a loose robe or vestments and pointed boots similar in style to those worn by the effigy of Conor *na Súiduine* [shoodhinna] O'Brien at Corcomroe. One hand holds a crozier and the other is raised in benediction. The third carved slab is a curious mixture of bas-relief with an attempt at intaglio at the neck. The figure has no headdress, wears a plain robe and round-toed footwear and carries a rectangular object, possibly a book, pressed close to the body. Inside the nave is a large stone font with scalloped carving similar to some of the carving found at Corcomroe.

Walking back along the lane that leads from the West Cross, the unusual stepped gable at the west end of the cathedral building is plain to see. It includes an internal staircase that may date in part to the thirteenth-century building. Also reused at the corners are carved capitals, similar in style to the capital above one of the mullions of the east window. The gable provoked the following contemptuous comment by a nineteenth-century visitor: 'The attempt at a tower is conspicuously mean and hideous. A pile of emigrants' luggage with a rabbit-hutch or bird-cage overhead would look equally imposing.'[27]

Looking at it on a hot, sunny day, it would not be difficult to imagine oneself viewing a church building in Mexico or Spain.

The Diocese of Kilfenora is small, and though it may have prospered for a time following its foundation, it declined in importance subsequently. By the early seventeenth century, it seems to have been so poor that nobody wanted to be appointed bishop. The perceived poverty of Kilfenora may be accounted for in part by different methods of assessing economic potential in the fourteenth and seventeenth centuries, but severe overgrazing through the Medieval period also reduced the livestock carrying capacity of the land.[28]

The Diocese of Kilfenora was united in 1750 with the Diocese of Kilmacduagh; both of these were, in turn, united with the Diocese of Galway in 1883. The establishment of the Church of Ireland church dates to 1837 and the parish is affiliated to the Church of Ireland Diocese of Killaloe. Today, the Bishop of Galway is Apostolic Administrator of the Catholic Diocese of Kilfenora. Technically, this means that he is not Bishop of Kilfenora, but administers the diocese on behalf of the Pope. This explains the significance of the banner displayed by the group from Kilfenora who attended the Papal mass in Dublin in 1979.

The Doorty Cross (Front)   The Doorty Cross (Back)

Monument Locations

GPS co-ordinates for all monument locations were compiled using a Garmin eTrex H hand-held device. The datum used for Irish grid references was 'Ireland 1965' and that for latitude and longitude was 'WGS 84'. Using other data or online mapping software may produce slight variations, but any differences will be marginal. Co-ordinates in the following table will guide the user to within a few metres of the monuments.

Name/Location	Type Irish	Grid	GPS
Ballynalackan Castle	Tower house	M 10366 00323	53°02'46.8"N 09°20'14.1"W
Caher Mór	Cashel	M 21995 04472	53°05'07.5"N 09°09'53.7"W
Cahercommaun	Cashel	R 28213 96501	53°00'52.9"N 09°04'13.2"W
Caherconnell	Cashel	R 23613 99491	53°02'27.3"N 09°08'22.4"W
Cahermacnaghten	Cashel	M 19671 00114	53°02'45.3"N 09°11'54.6"W
Cahermacnaghten	Law school	R 18912 99707	53°02'31.8"N 09°12'34.9"W
Carran	Church	R 23995 97375	53°01'19.0"N 09°08'00.2"W
Cnoc na Stúlaire	Enclosure	R 07627 96861	53°00'51.8"N 09°22'29.0"W
Corcomroe	Abbey	M 29496 08976	53°07'37.1"N 09°03'14.1"W
Creevagh	Wedge tomb	M 27260 95757	53°00'28.3"N 09°05'03.7"W
Doolin Axe Factory	Prehistoric site	R 06524 96469	53°00'39.8"N 09°23'36.2"W
Doolin Barrows	Ring barrows	R 06610 96081	53°00'27.7"N 09°23'30.8"W
Doonagore Castle	Tower house	R 06886 95690	53°00'14.0"N 09°23'12.2"W
Doonmacfelim Castle	Tower house	R 07108 96907	53°00'52.9"N 09°23'00.1"W
Drumcreehy	Church	M 24736 08620	53°07'23.1"N 09°07'29.9"W
Fahee North	Penitential stations	R 30995 99564	53°02'33.3"N 09°01'46.4"W
Fahee South	Fulacht fiadh	R 29188 98848	53°02'09.2"N 09°03'22.8"W
Glenaraha	Church	M 21218 04978	53°05'23.5"N 09°10'35.8"W
Gleninagh Castle	Tower house	M 19343 10321	53°08'15.2"N 09°12'21.4"W
Gleninagh Church	Church	M 19328 10091	53°08'07.8"N 09°12'22.0"W
Gleninsheen	Wedge tomb	M 22978 02158	53°03'53.2"N 09°08'58.9"W
Keelhilla	Fulacht fiadh	M 33017 03704	53°04'48.1"N 09°00'01.0"W
Kilcorney	Church	R 22460 99548	53°02'28.6"N 09°09'24.4"W
Kilfenora	Ecclesiastical site	R 18332 93996	52°59'26.7"N 09°13'00.8"W
Killilagh	Church	R 07789 97772	53°01'22.6"N 09°22'29.8"W
Killinaboy	Church	R 27108 91566	52°58'12.7"N 09°05'08.5"W
Leamaneh Castle	Tower/Fortified house	R 23484 93565	52°59'15.5"N 09°08'24.4"W
Muckinish (Muckinish Nua Castle)	Tower house	M 27716 09193	53°07'43.1"N 09°04'50.0"W
Muckinish (Seanmuckinish Castle)	Tower house	M 26258 10379	53°08'20.7"N 09°06'09.5"W
Newtown Castle	Tower house	M 21744 06531	53°06'14.0"N 09°10'09.0"W
Noughaval	Church	R 20830 96743	53°00'56.9"N 09°10'49.5"W
Oughtmama	Ecclesiastical site	M 30528 07854	53°07'00.7"N 09°02'18.0"W

Name/Location	Type Irish	Grid	GPS
Oughtmama (Tobar Cholmáin)	Holy well	M 31141 08182	53°07'11.6"N 09°01'44.8"W
Parknabinnia	Wedge tomb	R 26478 93575	52°59'17.3"N 09°05'43.9"W
Poulawack	Cashel	R 23329 98737	53°02'02.7"N 09°08'37.0"W
Poulawack	Cemetery cairn	R 23242 98529	53°01'56.0"N 09°08'41.6"W
Poulnabrone	Portal tomb	M 23605 00369	53°02'55.6"N 09°08'23.7"W
Rathborney	Church	M 20743 04736	53°05'15.4"N 09°11'01.2"W
St Mac Duagh's Hermitage	Ecclesiastical site	M 32885 04238	53°05'05.3"N 09°00'08.5"W
St Mac Duagh's Hermitage (Bóthar na Mias)	Legend	M 33287 04321	53°05'08.1"N 08°59'47.0"W
St Mac Duagh's Hermitage (servant's grave)	Ecclesiastical site	M 33306 04092	53°05'00.8"N 08°59'45.8"W
Templecronan	Church	M 28888 00002	53°02'46.4"N 09°03'39.6" W
Teergonean	Court tomb	R 06849 98469	53°01'44.7"N 09°23'20.8"W
The Rath	Ringfort	M 22417 04987	53°05'24.3"N 09°09'31.5"W
Tobar Fachtnan	Holy well	M 30041 00474	53°03'02.3"N 09°02'38.2"W
Tobar Fachtnan	Penitential stations	M 29985 00474	53°03'02.2"N 09°02'41.3"W
Toomullin	Church	R 08352 97085	53°01'01.8"N 09°21'54.5"W
Toomullin Castle	Tower house	R 08230 97160	53°01'03.9"N 09°21'59.0"W
Turlough Hill	Cairn	M 30326 06819	53°06'27.8"N 09°02'26.8"W
Turlough Hill	Hillfort	M 31415 07320	53°06'43.7"N 09°01'28.6"W
Turlough Hill	Settlement	M 30585 06950	53°06'31.6"N 09°02'14.1"W

Glossary

Antae	Projections of side walls beyond the gable.
Arris loop	*See* loop.
Barbican	A projecting guardroom over a castle gate.
Batter	A slope at the base of a wall.
Bawn	The area enclosed by a bawn wall.
Bawn wall	Fortification around a tower house or castle.
Brehon	An interpreter of the ancient Irish legal code known as Brehon Law.
Bullaun stone	A stone with a depression in which water can collect. Believed to have curative or magical powers.
Capital	The headstone of a column.
Cyclopean	Relating to a prehistoric Greek style of masonry using enormous, irregular stones.
Embrasure	The internally splayed recess of a door or window.
Fosse	A ditch, trench or moat.
Garderobe	Latrine.
Hanging eye	A hole, usually carved in stone, used to hold the upper pivot of a timber door.
Leacht	A memorial cairn; a grave-mound.
Loop	A vertical slit in a wall used as a window and an opening for defensive weapons. *Also* arrow-loop, gun-loop or loop-light. An arris loop is a similar slit in the angle of two walls.
Machicolation	A projecting section of a wall with a floor opening between supporting corbels through which missiles or waste could be dropped.
Midden	A refuse heap or dump.
Mullion	An upright division between the panes of a window.
Murder-hole	An opening in a ceiling through which missiles could be thrown or weapons fired at attackers.
Ogee	An S-shaped curve.
Ogham	An Early Medieval alphabet consisting of groups of scribed lines on either side of a base line. Usually scribed on stone.
Postern	A back gate in a bawn wall.

Putlog hole	A hole left behind in masonry after timber scaffolding supports have decayed.
Quoin	A corner stone.
Sedilia	Seats for the officiating clergy on the south side of the chancel. Usually three, and often built into a wall niche.
School of the West	A transitional late Romanesque/early Gothic architectural style of the early thirteenth century, characterised by expert carving and setting of feature windows in ashlar masonry.
Spall	A chip or splinter of stone.
Sheela-na-gig	A carving of a woman with exposed genitalia. Found on churches and castles, they were believed to offer protection against evil.
Souterrain	An underground passage or chamber. May have been used for refuge or storage.
Spandrel	The space between the curve of an arch and the outer frame or moulding.
Termon	A parcel of land around a church giving right of sanctuary.
Tower house	A stone residence of upper-class Gaelic and Anglo-Norman families, usually of 5–6 floors, built between c. AD 1400 and 1650.
Trabeate	Built of horizontal beams, as distinct from arches and vaults.
Tympanum	In an arched opening, the space between lintel and arch.
Voussoir	A wedge-like stone forming part of an arch.
Wall walk	A walkway inside the battlements of a castle or tower house.

Bibliography

Annála Connacht, Corpus of Electronic Texts. Cork: University College, Cork. Available at: http://www.ucc.ie/celt/published/T100011/index.html (Accessed 4 May 2010)

Annals of the Four Masters, Corpus of Electronic Texts. Cork: University College Cork. Available at: http://www.ucc.ie/celt/published/T100005E/index.html (Accessed 22 January 2011)

Baillie, M. G. L. (1995a), 'Dendrochronology and the Chronology of the Irish Bronze Age', Waddell, J. and Shee-Twohig, E. (eds.) *Ireland in the Bronze Age.* Dublin: The Stationery Office, pp. 30–37.

— (1995 b), *A Slice Through Time: Dendrochronology and Precision Dating.* London: Routledge.

Bredin, H. (2003), 'Suger (1081–1153) and Bernard of Clairvaux (1090–1153), Murray, C. (ed), *Key Writers on Art: From Antiquity to the Nineteenth Century.* London and New York: Routledge, pp. 28–33.

Breen, M. and Ua Cróinín, R. (2002), 'Some Restored Towerhouses in the Burren area of Co. Clare', *The Other Clare,* xxvi. Shannon: Shannon Archaeological & Historical Society, pp. 8–15.

— (2008), 'Towerhouses of the North Burren Coast', *The Other Clare,* xxxii, pp. 5–11.

Brindley, A. L. and Lanting, J. N. (1991–2), 'Radiocarbon Dates from the Cemetery at Poulawack, Co. Clare', *The Journal of Irish Archaeology,* vi. pp. 13–17.

Buckley, M. J. C. (1900), 'Notes on Boundary Crosses', *The Journal of the Royal Society of Antiquaries of Ireland, Fifth Series,* x. pp. 247–52. Available at: http://ia700104.us.archive.org/22/items/journalofroyalso30royauoft/journalofroyalso30royauoft.pdf (Accessed 11 January 2011)

Budd, P., Gale, D., Ixer, R. A. F., Thomas, R. G. (1994), 'Tin Sources for Prehistoric Bronze Production in Ireland', *Antiquity,* lxviii, 260, pp. 518–24.

Cahill, M. (2002), 'Before the Celts. Treasures in Gold and Bronze', Wallace, P. F. and Ó'Floinn, R. (eds.), *Treasures of the National Museum of Ireland.* Dublin: Gill & Macmillan, pp 86–124.

Comber, M. (ed.) (2000), *Folklore of Clare. A Folklore Survey of County Clare and County Clare Folk-Tales and Myths by T. J. Westropp*. Ennis: Clasp Press. (ed.) (2004), *Archaeology of the Burren. Prehistoric Forts and Dolmens in North Clare by T.J. Westropp*. Ennis: Clasp Press.

Comber, M. and Hull, G. (2010), 'Excavations at Caherconnell Cashel, the Burren, Co. Clare: Implications for Cashel Chronology and Gaelic Settlement', *Proceedings of the Royal Irish Academy, cx* (C), pp. 133–71.

Cooke, T. L. (1842–3), *Autumnal Rambles around New Quay, County Clare*. Galway: Galway Vindicator. Available at: http://www.clarelibrary. ie/eolas/coclare/history/autumnal_rambles/autumnal_rambles. htm. (Accessed 9 September 2010)

Cotter, C. (1999), 'Cahercommaun Fort, Co. Clare: A Reassessment of its Cultural Context', *Discovery Programme Reports v*, pp. 41–95.

Coxon, P. (1997), 'The Chilling Facts about Global Warming', *Technology Ireland,* xxix/3, pp. 16–19.

Cunningham, G. (1980), *Burren Journey West*. Limerick: Shannonside Mid-Western Regional Tourism Organisation.

Dennehy, E. (2008), 'Hot Property: The Morphology and Archaeology of the Irish Fulachta Fia', *Journal of the Kerry Archaeological and Historical Society, Series 2,*viii, pp. 5–27.

Dinneen, Rev P. S. (ed.) (1904), *Foclóir Gaedhilge agus Béarla. An Irish-English Dictionary, being a Thesaurus of the Words, Phrases and Idioms of the Modern Irish Language, with Explanations in English*. Dublin: M. H. Gill & Son; London: David Nutt.

Dwyer, P. (1878), *The Diocese of Killaloe from the Reformation to the close of the eighteenth century: with an appendix*. Dublin: Hodges, Foster and Figgis. Available at: http://www.archive.org/stream/ diocesekillaloe00dwyegoog#page/n516 (Accessed 7 September 2010)

— (1998), *A Handbook to Lisdoonvarna and its Vicinity*. Ennis: Clasp Press

Edwards, N. (1996), *The Archaeology of Early Medieval Ireland*. Oxford: Routledge.

Fitzpatrick, E. (2010), 'Excavations in the Law School Settlement of the O'Davoren Brehons', *Archaeology Committee Excavation Reports and Pictures*. Dublin: Royal Irish Academy. Available at: http:// www.ria.ie/our-work/committees/committees-for-the-humanities-

and-social-sciences/archaeology/excavation-reports---pictures.aspx. (Accessed 7 February 2011)

Frost, J. (1973), *The History and Topography of the County of Clare*. Dublin and Cork: The Mercier Press.

Feeser, I. and O'Connell, M. (2009), 'Fresh Insights' into Long-Term Changes in Flora, Vegetation, Land Use and Soil Erosion in the Karstic Environment of the Burren, Western Ireland', *Journal of Ecology*, xcvii/5, pp. 1083–1100.

Gilmore, H. (2009), 'Noughaval Church', *The Other Clare*, xxxiii, pp. 46–47.

Gosling, P. (1991), 'The Burren in Medieval Times', O'Connell, J. W. and Korff, A. (eds), *The Book of the Burren*. Kinvara: Tír Eólas, pp. 119–34.

Grattan Jr, H. (ed.) (1882), *The Speeches of the Right Honourable Henry Grattan in the Irish and the Imperial Parliament. ii.* Dublin: Longman, Hurst.

Haak, W, *et al.* (2005), 'Ancient DNA from the First European Farmers in 7,500-year-old Neolithic Sites', *Science*, cccx, 5750, pp. 1016–1018.

Harbison, P. (1976), 'The Double-Armed Cross on the Church Gable at Killinaboy, Co. Clare', *North Munster Antiquarian Journal*, xviii, pp. 3–12.

— (1996), 'Kilfenora', in 'The Limerick Area: Proceedings of the Royal Archaeological Institute', *Archaeological Journal*, cliii, pp. 340–45.

— (2000a) 'The Church of Rath Blathmac – A Photo-essay', *The Other Clare*, xxiv, pp. 23–31.

— (2000b) 'An Ancient Pilgrimage "Relic Road" in North Clare?', *The Other Clare*, xxiv, pp. 55–59.

Hearn, M. F. (1985), *Romanesque Sculpture: The Revival of Monumental Stone Sculpture in the Eleventh and Twelfth Centuries*. Ithaca: Cornell University Press.

Hencken, H. O'N. (1938), *Cahercommaun: A Stone Fort in County Clare*. Dublin: The Royal Society of Antiquaries of Ireland.

Itan, Y., Powell, A., Beaumont, M. A., Burger, J. and Thomas, M. G.

—(2009), 'The Origins of Lactase Persistence in Europe', *Computational Biology*, v/8, e1000491. Available at: http://www.ploscompbiol. org/article/info:doi%2F10.1371%2Fjournal.pcbi.1000491. (Accessed 9 September 2010)

Jones, C. (2004), *The Burren and the Aran Islands. Exploring the Archaeology.* Cork: The Collins Press.

Joyce, P. W. (1869), *The Origin and History of Irish Names of Places.* Dublin: McGlashan & Gill. Available at: http://www.archive.org/details/originhistoryofi01joycuoft. (Accessed 14 January 2011)

Lavelle, D. (1994), 'Newtown Castle, Newtown. 1994:20'. *Database of Irish Excavation Reports.* Available through: http://www.excavations. ie/Pages/HomePage.php. (Accessed 2 October 2010.)

Lewis, S. (1995), *A History and Topography of County Clare.* Ennis: Clasp Press.

Lucas, A. (2006), *Wind, Water, Work: Ancient and Medieval Milling Technology.* Oxford: Oxbow Books.

Mac Mahon, M. (2000), 'The Cult of Inghin Bhaoith and the Church of Killinaboy', *The Other Clare,* xxiv, pp. 12–17.

MacNamara, N. C. (1999 reprint of 1896 edition), *The Story of an Irish Sept: the Origins and History of the MacNamaras.* Ruan: Martin Breen.

MacNamara, G. U. (1907), 'Kilnaboy (recte, Cill Inghin Bháith), Co. Clare', *Journal of the Royal Society of Antiquaries of Ireland,* xxxvii/4, Miscellanea.

Moran, P. F. (1911). 'St. Palladius', *The Catholic Encyclopedia.* New York: Robert Appleton Company. Available at: http://www.newadvent. org/cathen/11424a.htm (Accessed 30 June 2009)

Nelson, E. C. and Stalley, R. A. (1989), 'Medieval Naturalism and the Botanical Carvings at Corcomroe Abbey (County Clare)', Gesta, xxviii/2, pp. 165–74.

Ní Ghabhláin, S. (1995), 'Church and Community in Medieval Ireland: The Diocese of Kilfenora', *The Journal of the Royal Society of Antiquaries of Ireland,* cxxv, pp. 61–84.

Nugent, P. (2007), *The Gaelic Clans of County Clare and their Territories, 1100–1700 A.D.* Dublin: Geography Publications.

O'Brien, I. (1986), *O'Brien of Thomond. The O'Briens in Irish History, 1500 – 1865.* Chichester: Phillimore & Co.

O'Donovan, J. and O'Curry, E. (1839), *Ordnance Survey Letters.* Available through: http://www.clarelibrary.ie/eolas/coclare/history/osl/ index.htm (Accessed 7 September 2010)

O'Murchadha, C. (1991), 'The Richest Commoner in Ireland. Sir Donough O'Brien of Leamaneh and Dromoland, Baronet. (1842–1717)', *Dál gCais: The Journal of Clare,* x, pp. 7–12.

Peck, H. T. (1898), *Harpers Dictionary of Classical Antiquities.* New York. Harper and Brothers. Available at: http://www.chlt.org/sandbox/perseus/harper/page.3154.a.php?size=240x320. (Accessed 8 August 2010)

Raftery, B. (1994), Pagan Celtic Ireland: *The Enigma of the Irish Iron Age,* London: Thames and Hudson.

Stalley, R. (1987), *The Cistercian Monasteries of Ireland.* London and New Haven: Yale University Press.

Stout, M. (1997), *The Irish Ringfort.* Dublin: Four Courts Press.

Swan, D. L. (1991), 'The Churches, Monasteries and Burial Grounds of The Burren', O'Connell, J. W. and Korff, A. (eds.), *The Book of the Burren.* Kinvara: Tír Eólas, pp. 95–118.

Swinfen, A. (1992), *Forgotten Stones: Ancient Church Sites of The Burren and Environs.* Dublin: Lilliput Press.

Tacitus, P. C. (1877 edition, translated by Church, A. J. and Brodribb, W. J.), *Agricola.* London: Macmillan, Chapter 24 available at: http://www.forumromanum.org/literature/tacitus/agricola_e.html#24 (Accessed 7 August 2010)
The Placenames Database of Ireland. Available at: http://logainm.ie (Accessed 12 September 2010)

Waddell, J. (2000), *The Prehistoric Archaeology of Ireland.* Bray: Wordwell.

Warner, R., Chapman, R., Cahill, M. and Moles, N. (2009), 'The Gold Source Found at Last?', *Archaeology Ireland,* xxiii/2, pp. 22–25.

Westropp, T. J. (1899), 'Notes on the Lesser Castles or "Peel Towers" of the County Clare', *Proceedings of the Royal Irish Academy* 1889–1901, v, pp. 348–65.

(1900) 'The Churches of County Clare, and the Origin of the Ecclesiastical Divisions in That County', *Proceedings of the Royal Irish Academy,* vi, pp. 100–80.

—(1905), 'The Coast of County Clare', *Illustrated Guide to the Northern, Western and Southern Islands and Coast of Ireland,* Royal Society of Antiquaries of Ireland Antiquarian Handbook Series, vi, Dublin: Hodges Figgis and Co. pp. 97–116. Available at: http://www.archive.org/stream/illustratedguid00irelgoog (Accessed 14 January 2011)

— (1907), 'Lemeneagh Castle, County Clare', *Journal of the Royal Society of Antiquaries in Ireland,* xxxvii/4, Miscellanea, p. 411.

Notes

Introduction
1. Dinneen, 1904; Joyce, 1896, 381

Part 1

1. The Archaeological Ages
1. Coxon, 1997
2. Itan *et al*, 2009, 6
3. Haak *et al*, 2005, 1017
4. Dunne, N., personal communication, Waddell, 2000, 37
5. Jones, 2004, 63
6. *Ibid.*, 51
7. Feeser & O'Connell, 2009, 1098
8. Baillie, 1995 (a)
9. Dunne, N., personal communication
10. Baillie, 1995 (b), 83
11. Waddell, 2000, 118
12. Budd *et al.*, 1994
13. Cahill, 2002, 90
14. Warner *et al.*, 2009
15. Dunne, N., personal communication
16. Raftery, 1994, 37
17. *Ibid.*, 113
18. Tacitus, 1877 edition
19. Moran, 1911
20. Edwards, 1996, 103
21. Dowd, forthcoming
22. Dwyer, 1878, 62
23. Swan, 1991, 104–5
24. Edwards, 1996, 128
25. Buckley, 1900, 248

Part 2

2. Burren East

1. MacNamara, 1907, 406
2. For a further discussion of the name, see Mac Mahon, 2000.
3. Harbison, 1976, 4 and 2000 (b), 58
4. Harbison, 2000 (b)
5. Dwyer, 1878, 494
6. *Loc. cit.*
7. *Loc. cit.*
8. O'Donovan and O'Curry, 1839, 12
9. Comber, 2000, 57
10. Swinfen, 1992, 75
11. Dwyer, *op. cit.*, 92
12. *Ibid.*, 362–63
13. Hencken, 1938
14. Cotter, 1999, 49
15. *Ibid.*
16. Dennehy, 2008, 14
17. See also Harbison, 2000 (a), 26, Fig. H
18. *The Placenames Database of Ireland,* 104326

3. Burren North

1. Comber, 2004, 114
2. Peck, 1898, 452
3. Westropp, 1905, 102
4. Cooke, 1842, X
5. Jones, 2004, 89–90
6. Lucas, 2006, 36, Note 50
7. Cooke, *loc. cit.*
8. O'Donovan and O'Curry, 1839, 30
9. Stalley, 1987, 108
10. *Annála Connacht,* 1228.16
11. Bredin, 2003, 30
12. Nelson and Stalley, 1989, 165

13. Hearn, 1985, 52; Stalley, op. cit., 15
14. Westropp, 1905, 99
15. Breen and Ua Cróinín, 2008, 9
16. Mac Namara, 1999 reprint, 205
17. O'Donovan and O'Curry, op. cit., 25
18. Westropp, 1900, 130; Westropp, 1905, 99; Swinfen, 1992, 18
19. Ní Ghabhláin, 1995, 79
20. Lewis, 1995, 38
21. Cooke, 1842, I
22. Ní Ghabhláin, *op. cit.*, 74
23. Cooke, *loc. cit.*
24. Ní Ghabhláin, *op. cit.*, 73, 77
25. O'Donovan and O'Curry, *op. cit.*, 66
26. Cooke, *loc. cit.*
27. Cunningham, 1980, 42; Breen and Ua Cróinín, 2002, 11
28. Reproduced in Frost, 1973, 20
29. Frost, *op. cit.*, 24
30. O'Donovan and O'Curry, *op. cit.*, 26
31. Lavelle, 1994
32. Grattan, 1882, 100
33. Lewis, *op. cit.*, 118

4. Burren West

1. Westropp, 1899, 355
2. Annals of the Four Masters, 1585.26
3. Comber, 2004, 130
4. O'Donovan and O'Curry, 1839, 103
5. Jones, 2004, 46
6. Frost, 1973, Appendix
7. Comber, op. cit., 129
8. *Ibid.*, 126–7
9. Gosling, 1991, 130
10. Reproduced in Dwyer, 1878, 219
11. O'Brien, 1986, 187

5. Burren Central

1. Jones, 2004, 51–54
2. Gosling, 1991, 130
3. Westropp, 1907, 411
4. O'Murchadha, 1991, 8
5. Westropp, 1900, 134
6. *Ibid.*, 116
7. Gosling, forthcoming
8. O'Donovan and O'Curry, 1839, 32
9. Joyce, 1869, 382
10. Brindley and Lanting, 1991–2, 17
11. O'Donovan and O'Curry, *op. cit.*, 62, footnote 5
12. Ní Ghabhláin, 1995, 81
13. Comber, 2004, 47; Westropp, 1900, 133
14. Ní Ghabhláin, *op. cit.*, 79
15. Comber and Hull, 2010, 136, 158
16. Comber, 2004, 47, note 2
17. Lewis, 1995, 60
18. Stout, 1997, 24
19. Comber, 2004, 54
20. *Annála Connacht,* 1364.8
21. Fitzpatrick, 2010
22. Gilmore, 2009, 46
23. Comber, 2000, 56
24. Comber, 2004, 23
25. Joyce, *op. cit.*, 24–26
26. Harbison, 1996
27. Dwyer, 1998, 59
28. Nugent, 2007, 106